The Vanishing Hero

The Vanishing Hero

Studies in Novelists of the Twenties

by

SEAN O'FAOLAIN

Essay Index Reprint Series

 BOOKS FOR LIBRARIES PRESS
FREEPORT, NEW YORK

PR
888
.H4
O3

The chapter on Virginia Woolf and James
Joyce first appeared in *New World Writing*
No. 10.

INTERNATIONAL STANDARD BOOK NUMBER:
0-8369-2065-1

LIBRARY OF CONGRESS CATALOG CARD NUMBER:
71-142686

PRINTED IN THE UNITED STATES OF AMERICA

Author's Note

IN THE spring of 1953 I was invited to give six lectures at Princeton University as part of the Christian Gauss Seminars in Criticism. I have here expanded them into a book on the basis of further thought and the constructive comments of my listeners — or, as I prefer to think of them, my colleagues — during the, to me at least, valuable discussions that followed each lecture. I take this opportunity to express my warmest thanks to everybody who made my stay at Princeton such a pleasant three months; especially to the organizers of the seminars and the Rockefeller Foundation, who made my visit, those lectures and this book possible.

Contents

THE FERVENT TWENTIES

THE novelists here dealt with were all, with the exception of Joyce, novelists of the twenties. Virginia Woolf alone had published before 1920. Aldous Huxley's first novel appeared in that year; Miss Bowen's first stories in 1923; Waugh's first novel, *Decline and Fall,* in 1928; Greene's *The Man Within* in 1929. The period attracted me for three reasons. I wanted to examine some of the basic assumptions of the novel in our time; I had formed an idea that the twenties are a watershed or divide in the history of the contemporary novel; and it offered a group of writers with a large or completed body of work, of some variety and evident distinction. The only reason why I did not go on to consider more novelists of the period was that I was confined to six lectures, and I thought it better to concentrate in each lecture on one writer. Originally I did not deal with Aldous Huxley at all, feeling that satire was sufficiently covered by Waugh, and suspecting what I have since decided is true, that Huxley is not, properly speaking, a satirist so much as a writer of brilliant invective.

I did not attempt to systematize the conclusions that presented themselves to me as I reread these novelists. I feared to be tempted by the appeal of a schematical argument into forcing a theory instead of accumulating what I hoped would end up as an informative review of a literary period. But the theme did begin to force itself — that the central assumption of the contemporary novel, the one constant in all the writers before me, is the virtual disappearance from fiction of that focal character of the classical novel, the conceptual Hero. As so often happens, the end of the journey now finds itself in the prospectus, these prefatory pages.

As I see the matter, the Hero, as we commonly try to use the word and the idea, is a purely social creation. He represents, that is to say, a socially approved norm, for representing which to the satisfaction of society he is decorated with a title. The traditional novel — the term "traditional" will have to be considered and qualified later on — had always moved about this socially acceptable character, so that even when he was not visibly or obtrusively present, as in *Les Liaisons Dangereuses* or *Manon Lescaut,* a form of lip service was given to his hovering spirit by at least a final, formal admission that "crime does not pay." The Hero was on the side of the long arm of the law, the *Sûreté,* the church, the kirk, the headmaster and the head of the family. He was on the side of Squire Allworthy, Mr. John Knightley, Père Goriot, Mrs. Proudie and Sherlock Holmes, or at least he was after he had been permitted a certain license to roam in order to entertain us, and had duly returned to the bosom of conventional behavior, as, for example, young Chuzzlewit returned,

after "Eden" had reformed him, to the bosom of Mary Graham. Naturally some of the best novelists always kicked
against this social convention, much to the satisfaction of the
reading public and to the annoyance of the social critics; as
happened to Scott when he wrote *Rob Roy* about a free-
booter and Fielding when he wrote *Tom Jones* about a ras-
cal. "A hero," cried Thackeray, of Tom Jones, somewhat
hypocritically, one fears, "with a flawed reputation, a hero
sponging for a guinea, a hero who cannot pay his landlady,
and is obliged to let his honour out to hire, is absurd, and the
claim of Tom Jones to heroic rank is quite untenable." The
reference to the landlady is the revealing item in the list. No
man could be a hero if he was so antisocial as not to pay his
debts.

The Hero, and his opposite number, the Villain, represented in the traditional novel conflicts which they more or
less clearly defined. That was in those good old days when
novelists were prepared to accept the fact that certain current ideas expressed firmly and clearly what the majority of
people meant by a good or wholesome life. The novelist
might not subscribe fully to these ideas or ideals himself; he
might feel critical about them, poke fun at them, even reject
them in his heart; but he could not deny that they formed
the basis of the society in which he lived and which he
described, and that anybody who rebelled against them,
whether in real life or in fiction, must find himself not only
in conflict with his community but in conflict with his origins
and probably with his own nature. In admitting so much he
admitted the social concept of Heroism. If the novelist were
a Stevenson, a Thackeray or a Dickens his readers knew
where they were, and where the author stood, immediately

they had identified the Hero. But the identification was not always so easy, especially with the French novelists. Many readers of the Abbé Prévost's entertaining account of the career of Manon Lescaut must have closed the book in a somewhat puzzled frame of mind as to the Abbé's convictions, in spite of his effort to clarify his position in the last few pages by bringing disaster on the head of his heroine. Even here, however, one thing at least was clear: Manon, like all other such strays from the narrow path, was agin the government, and she was therefore in a very proper danger of life and happiness. This would have soothed the Abbé's readers and increased their ambivalent pleasure in reading of her adventures. On the other hand, the first readers of de Laclos's *Les Liaisons Dangereuses* (1782) can have been in no doubt that his was a thoroughly subversive book in so far as it denied all social and moral values. It is, perhaps, the first European novel without a social Hero. Its rank as a masterpiece forces us to note that the term "traditional novel" does not exclude rivals, exceptional in more senses than one, whose increasing effect from the seventeenth century on was to put the social concept of the Hero more and more on the defensive until it was finally overthrown completely.

II

The struggle, though it was not immediately apparent, began early. Even in the seventeenth century we are sensible of the insidious intrusion of other and less moral values; which is, no doubt, no more than one would expect of a period governed overtly by rigid laws and conventions but se-

cretly as licentious as any other. After all, the central seventeenth-century classical idea of *amour-vertu* — the idea, or
the hope, that once man beheld the Good he must naturally
love it — not only did not exclude the basic fact of natural
desire but by definition emphasized it. For *amour-vertu*, seen
as that force which builds the soul's perfection (*cette puis-
sance d'ajouter à la perfection de nos âmes*), not only implies
imperfection but implies also that imperfection is a highly
attractive thing against which the soul has to struggle long
and painfully. (There could be no drama at all otherwise.)
This in turn implies something even more important to our
immediate interest — that both the writer and the public
were enormously interested in the emotional tug-of-war between the "soul" and "imperfection." So, for instance, although in the great novel of the century before de Laclos,
Madame de Lafayette's *La Princesse de Clèves,* virtue triumphs over weakness, the contemporary reader may or not
have been vicariously relieved, but he could not have meantime been much interested if his sympathies had not been
engaged and the struggle long in doubt. A certain ambivalence, one perceives, thereby enters into the novel, dividing
admiration and sympathy, virtue and pleasure.

Sympathy thus opened the first assault on the social code,
and on the Hero who represented it. If one's sympathy for
human unhappiness begins to dominate one's moral sense,
the senses, the stern moralist will maintain, must end by dom-
inating both. "Man," says Cousin, in his *Philosophie du xviii
Siècle,* "is a creature who naturally finds the unhappiness
of others hard to bear; to blot out the sight of unhappiness
he is, so to speak, obliged to collaborate with the unhappy."
The result is that virtue and happiness soon become coter-

minous and "the words goodness and beauty agree to define
whatever qualities add to our pleasure in anything . . ."; in
the end, "anything that soothes the passions ends by being
called 'good.'" On this basis the sensibilities began, little by
little, to impose a new set of values on the old.

Yet it only happened little by little, ambiguously and inex-
plicitly, and nothing was overtly admitted or acknowledged.
Readers of, say, the sentimental novels of Crebillon might,
when the heroine yields to passion, water her burning heart
with their tears, dare to feel that love is the only true criterion
of joy, even go so far as to hold that *l'amour doit détruire tous
les préjugés* (should override all prejudices); but they still
had to admit — because it was so — that the whole tragedy
and tension of illicit love lay in the fact that the dictates of
established society (*les préjugés*) were opposed to these lawless dictates of the heart and would inevitably condemn and
destroy those who dared yield to them. The reader, to put
it in a vulgar way, got his fun out of the Hero's sense of
tension; rather in the manner of a spectator at a bullfight
who gets his "fun" out of the matador's tensions. The interest
to us here is that, imperceptibly, the Hero and the Villain
are changing sides, though nobody will yet admit it. The
spectator ought to be on the side of the bull — symbol of
society, tradition, the good earth, the herd, the life-giver, the
head of the family; he gets his pleasure instead, or some of
his pleasure, in watching the bull-baiter. But, then, being
himself a bull, a head of a family, a one-of-the-herd, a social
man, he must, at the end, when the bull-baiter is gored by
the bull, lean back, close the book, and say aloud for the
benefit of his attendant family: "Well, of course, yes! One
should not bait bulls." In other words, the readers' and the

novelists' ambivalence increases. Society is cruel. Society is even to be criticized. Society . . . But nobody will go quite so far as to reverse traditional roles and say that society is the villain of the piece.

L'Abbé Prévost certainly did not dare say so, though he did by playing on the sensibilities of his readers tempt them to think so. Indeed, he is more than evasive about it all, as when, washing his hands over his *L'Homme de Qualité,* he says, surely not without some hypocrisy: *"Les coeurs sensibles, les esprits raisonnables, tous ceux, en un mot, qui — sans suivre une philosophie trop sévère — ont du goût pour la vertu, la sagesse, et la vérité, pourront trouver quelque plaisir dans la lecture de cet ouvrage."* (Every sensitive heart, every rational spirit, in a word, everybody who — *without yielding to too severe a philosophy of life* — has a feeling for virtue, wisdom and truth, will find some pleasure in the perusal of this work.) Not that the public was not occasionally more frank, as witness this kind of remark from a review of Prévost's *Manon Lescaut* (1733): "Manon is an interesting creation. She may deceive her lover twenty times; it does not matter. She is unfaithful, yet never perfidious. She continues to love her adoring knight. Because of that love we forgive her everything." *

Rousseau is quite another pair of sleeves. The Abbé Prévost made no attempt to teach, or point a moral, or state a social problem. He neither had time for it in these novels of adventure, nor — here in full keeping with the traditions of the novel of feeling — were such matters his main interest.

---

* *L'Année littéraire,* 1784, p. 107 seq. Quoted in *Le Genre Romanesque en France depuis l'apparition de la* Nouvelle Héloïse *jusqu'aux approches de la Révolution.* Gervais Étienne. Paris, 1922.

His main interest was in the personages whose fates attracted him. *La Nouvelle Héloïse* (1761), on the other hand, has been well described by Lanson as *"un rêve de volupté re-dressé en instruction morale"* — a dream of happiness de-voted to the purposes of moral teaching. Unfortunately, most readers of Rousseau's novel remember only the first part, in which Julie becomes the lover of Saint Preux, and forget, or never even read, the second part, in which she is presented as the faithful wife of Wolmar, whom she does not love. Perhaps they forget, too, that the whole point of the novel is that it is a fictional representation of the essential burthen of the Social Contract — which is that while nature made men happy and society makes them unhappy *la nature humaine ne rétrograde pas* (human nature cannot go back). Social living has its own charms and triumphs, and all that men in society can now do is to recover certain attributes of primitive life, such as innocence and liberty. So, while Julie and Saint Preux do not sin against nature, they do sin against society; but society, by insisting rigidly on moral behavior, in turn presses Julie so hard that it also sins by making it well-nigh impossible for her not to transgress. Her dilemma thus poses, once more, and for the first time intelligently, that antagonism between the person and the social group which earlier novels were content to evoke by the appeal to feelings of pity.

De Laclos (his novel appeared twenty-one years later: 1782) is uncompromising. Mme. de Merteuil and Valmont, enemies of society and of each other, would have found in Julie's faithfulness to Wolmar nothing but another delightful incentive towards inflicting a new defeat on society by cor-rupting her — another blow, that is, for the social idea that

love makes demands on honor, and that honor respects the
social structure erected on the basis of faithful love. The Age
of Reason has not only arrived but gone too far in *Les
Liaisons Dangereuses,* or rather in the behavior of its two
active ingredients — whom one cannot well call its Hero and
Heroine since they are, at bottom, opposed to everything still
inherent in those two words. This is well put by Martin
Turnell: "The eighteenth century *philosophes* had no difficulty in continuing the work of the seventeenth century and
in completing the destruction of moral sanctions on the rational plane. . . . The Man of Honour and the Man of Passion had had their day and disappeared from the scene.
Laclos' theme is the tragedy of the Rational Man, the man
who was carefully conditioned through the removal of all
moral scruples and the sense of guilt, but inevitably condemned to action in a very limited field. The novel is a masterpiece because it gives final expression to this phase of
human experience."

Still, it could only be a phase. De Merteuil and Valmont
are indeed, by being enemies of society, limited in their
scope and possible ambitions. Their lives as corrupters of
virtue are lived on the periphery of normalcy. They have
the freedom only of gangsters, brigands, cutthroats or pick-
pockets. As Turnell says so vividly, these people are always
whispering. Yet they foreshadow in their limited and corrupt
way something immensely important: the fact that, since
sniping at the world is hardly a full-time occupation, any
man of real ambition must either decide to be part of
the world of accepted values and rise to power within its
framework, or else decide to conquer it. We are on the
threshold of the age of Napoleon, the age of the man of

ambition, of energy, of dreams all his very own. The novelists who, like Prévost, had concentrated on the interest of individual emotions will now concentrate on the individual in action — and probably in active revolt. The social Hero is about to discover that his opposite number is not the Villain but himself imbued by new and disturbing forms of discontent.

The first real flag of revolt was the romantic's angry and agonized cry of distress at the cruelty of society in Benjamin Constant's *Adolphe* (1816). It is lucid and unillusioned. It paints not the ecstasies of irregular love but its inevitable and continuing misery. From start to finish Adolphe and Ellénore are torn by unhappiness, and the great merit of this little masterpiece of doomed passion is in its clear realization that things could not have gone otherwise. In the Epilogue the author is explicit. All ambivalence is dissipated:

> The story of Ellénore's tragedy shows that the most passionate feeling cannot prevail against the established order. The power of society is strong and takes too many shapes. It pours bitterness and gall into the sort of love whose existence it refuses to admit. It encourages inconstancy and ennui, twin maladies which take the soul unawares in the very heart and center of love. In the name of morality the poor-in-spirit sow discord, and in their zeal for virtue they sow evil. It is as if because they themselves are incapable of love they hate the sight of it and under any possible pretext revel in attacking it and destroying it. . . . Society arms itself with everything that is mean and evil in the human heart to destroy whatever is good in it.

The only words of condemnation are those which insist that Adolphe's virtues were not founded on principles but on emotions, so that all he is left with in the end are the memories of his unkindness to Ellénore.

With Balzac the novel frees itself from the limited scope of fated passion and the subjective obsession with affairs of the heart. The Napoleonic inspiration is here at its fullest voltage. The mark of it throughout his work is his enormous admiration for pure energy. For example, this kind of excited outburst: *"Il n'y a plus énergie à Paris. Un poignard est une curiosité qu'on suspend à un clou doré."* (But there is no energy any more in Paris. Here a dagger is simply a curio that we hang on the wall on a gilded nail.) And so on: "Now, in Italy everything is much more clear-cut! There the women are ravening animals, dangerous sirens, following no other logic, responding to no other reasons than their appetites and their hungers. You have to be as careful with them as you would with tigresses." (Though this may be also an echo of the contemporary admiration for *Robinson Crusoe*, the modern myth of man's conquest of wild nature.) For Balzac, man *must* conquer something. That has been in the air of France ever since the Corsican made all Frenchmen feel that man is a free creature with no limits to his ambition but those of his own audacity. Accordingly, to Balzac the man of ruthless and amoral ambition is the proper man to take center stage and his novels are full of such men. True, something of the usual ambiguity and ambivalence still creeps in to confuse the issue a little — such as pious platitudes about the need to preserve church and state; sentiments more or less sincerely felt according as Balzac's own efforts to make a place for himself in the *haute monde* succeed or flag — but the general effect is unmistakably that of a struggle between ruthless individual ambition and what is sometimes nowadays called in Britain the "Establishment."

One could cull from his novels many observations to enforce this impression, along the lines of this sentence from the *Médecin de Campagne*: "*Le contrat social sera toujours un pacte perpetuel entre ceux qui possèdent contre ceux qui ne possèdent pas.*" (The Social Contract will always be a pact between those who have against those who have not.) Where, here, one asks, is the Hero? On which side is he in this? Victim or accomplice? Which is Rastignac, the ambitious young gallant of *Père Goriot?* Social Hero? Or rebellious brigand? What are we to think when we are told that the experience of any young man, such as Rastignac, coming to Paris to make his way in the world must be to see vice successful and virtue mocked (*la vertu persiflé*)? Are we to anticipate that the Balzacian hero will take the side of virtue? We are told in fact that "the young man begins to totter, his will and his conscience become divorced, and" — here is a typical piece of ambivalence, a moral observation from a novelist who is scarcely *preaching* morality — "the infernal work of demoralization is soon complete." But the moral observation does not succeed in impressing us. Every novelist reveals his sympathies by his obsessions. He cannot, by throwing in a moral observation, imagine he has then made a fair counterbalance of justice. Balzac, thinking of his own struggles, ambitions and failures, and projecting them in men like Rastignac, is constantly evoking sympathy for ambitious men by the very passion of his intensity in depicting them.

The views he makes them express, though not necessarily his views, vibrate with a force which is his force. So, at the

beginning of the *Maison Nucingen* — which begins where
Père Goriot left off — the narrator (Balzac) overhears a
group of dandies discussing Rastignac's rise to fortune. Their
comments, which are Balzac's invention, are not necessarily
his opinions, but he does nothing to contradict them and he
does much to make them plausible or at least palatable to
the reader. The burthen of the story is put into Bixion's
mouth: "Rastignac, from the moment of his debut in Paris,
looked at society with a skeptical eye. From 1820 onward
he thought, just like the baron, that honest men are so only
in appearance and he therefore saw the world as a blend of
every kind of corruption and deceit. He admitted that there
were individual exceptions, but he condemned the majority
of men. He denied the existence of virtue, though he admitted that in certain circumstances men do display it. This
decision was arrived at in a single moment. He acquired his
knowledge of the world on the hilltop of Père Lachaise the
day he buried there that poor, honest man who had been the
father of his Delphine, who died, abandoned by his daughters and his sons-in-law, the dupe of society and of his own
sincere feelings. He decided there and then to play the
world's game, to assume the mantle of virtue, of honesty, of
fine sentiments, while in fact clothing himself from head to
foot in the armor of his own egoism. . . ."

The implication is that Rastignac did well because he did
successfully. This becomes clear when we cast our minds
back from this summary to the last dramatic and poignant
scene of *Père Goriot* where the old man is being buried in
Père Lachaise, and recall his sacrifices for his daughters, and
Rastignac's earlier naïvetés and sufferings, and the rude contrast with Vautrin's ruthless schemings. We must see then

how sardonically the Grand Design of the *Comédie Humaine*
underlines the word *comedy,* if only by pointing out that the
heroes whom society acclaims are not all as admirable either
as society pretends or imagines them to be. Rastignac in the
cemetery had not had, we remember, a coin with which to
pay the gravediggers. "As he looked down at the grave he
dropped into it the last tear of his youth." Then he moved
up to the higher part of the cemetery and looked down at
the glittering lights of Paris, darted glance after glance over
its humming hive, and said: "Now for our turn! Hers and
mine!" Then — "as a first challenge to society, he went to
dine with Madame de Nucingen." It is the final line of the
novel.

It may evoke another rebel of a very different metal and
another ambition, also proposing to conquer in Paris — young
Stephen Daedalus. But the differences are immense. Rastignac seeks to conquer the world; Daedalus abandons all
hope of it to conquer himself; the ambition of the one is
material, of the other metaphysical; the one is a rebel, the
other is a martyr; and where Byron would have admired
both, Shelley would have admired Daedalus the more; as
for Rastignac as man of energy and action — he would
have considered Daedalus either a fool, or one of the world's
few exceptions to the almost universal rule that the only
thing that makes men toil is self-interest, and that their only
reward is its satisfaction.

With Stendhal the destruction of the Social Hero is completed. Stendhal's concept of the spur and the reward of toil
is the refinement of Balzac in proportion as he deals in finer
spirits, has a more lyrical view of life, a more lucid though
less robust intelligence and is, in sum, the superior writer

of the two. After all, while Julien Sorel realizes that he must either conquer the world or be conquered by it, become a Napoleon or — as he does — end on the gallows, his aim is not just success, pleasure or power but, ultimately, to satisfy his own ego and to prove an idea: that life is to those who dare to live it. This intrusion of a subjective note marks Stendhal as the true father of the modern anti-Hero, who is almost always subjective, and one might dare say *therefore* always a failure. For life is not to those who dare to live it if, in effect, they live it as much within their minds as Julien, and apparently as Stendhal did before and after him. That famous scene in *Le Rouge et le Noir* (1831), where Julien decides to prove himself to himself by taking the hand of the mayoress at a certain moment by the clock, reveals the flaw in the theory: for Julien does take her hand, and from that moment he does believe in his own audacity — but what has happened to the hand of the mayoress? If a man loves not for love's sake but for an idea's sake where has "living" gone to? In effect Julien, like Madame de Merteuil before him in *Les Liaisons Dangereuses*, tends to kill every emotional experience by subserving it to ends other than itself.

But this is one of the main differences between the art of Balzac (and of all who went before him and carried on his tradition after him) and the art of Stendhal and of all those who are of *his* tradition: that Balzac aims to re-create the objective world in terms of its own actual, tangible, verifiable truth — admittedly, inevitably as the writer sees it or interprets it — whereas Stendhal aims to express his own personal, subjective truth in terms of the objective world. The heroes of Balzac are men of the world; the heroes of Stendhal are men who want to be men of the world. Neither type of hero really accepts the world in which he moves or towards which he is drawn; but because of his gift of irony Stendhal is much more lucid about it all than Balzac, whose heroes are forever weltering in the thick of the battle.

One might say that, of the two, Stendhal is the greater anarchist, simply because he is so devastatingly lucid. When Count Mosca in *La Chartreuse de Parme* (1839) tells young Fabrizio that it is silly to complain about the rules and conventions of the world, of society or of politics, considering that one does not complain about the rules of the game of whist, could moral subversion go farther? If one "plays the game" in this sense of the term, nothing, it is evident, is left of social morality but whatever natural, innate decency there may be in the individual sufficiently endowed to be able to play the game with skill and grace. The Hero then becomes, it is surely obvious, not society's Hero but society's secret exploiter. If he succeeds, he becomes his own private Hero, applauded by nobody else, possibly even visible as such to nobody else. At that point the old terms Hero and Heroine, though they may go on being used through idle habit, no longer have any general validity or clear meaning as far as fiction is concerned; while as for what is called "real life," they will continue to be applicable publicly only for so long as large masses of people are ready to believe that any man who acts bravely in their cause is a heroic character, whereas men acting as bravely for some contrary cause are not. Such a usage equally ignores the fact that the word *heroic*, or *heroism*, can therefore have so little moral content that the public "hero" may be a private "villain." (There are, of course, many other examples of life outmoding language in this way: for instance the continuing use of the now almost meaningless title Liberal.) It would be difficult to show this process at work in the English novel at any period; impossible over the same period. The whole English idea of society was that it was a system to be accepted; it was a game played so instinctively that nobody realized that it was a game. Nobody stood outside the thing and observed it analytically, so that English literature lacks the French cutting-edge until we come to Wilde and Shaw; and Shaw, we note, is a critic of social problems rather than individual crises. There are one or two swallows: one could build something on Becky Sharp as a likable *corsaire;* on the victim-heroines of the Brontës; on Trollope's angry reactions to the spites and compressions of small-town society — but there is, as one might say, no party line within the English novel to suggest that other concepts of the Hero are burrowing underneath it. We are almost on the threshold of the twentieth century before we observe English novelists begin to take on something of the individualistic spirit of the French; and the same naturally applies to the novel in America.

Neither have I attempted, nor am I fitted to discuss the underlying reasons for this disintegration of the social Hero. All I have done is to mention several novels from well behind our century which show that the process has been going on a long time. What the ultimate reasons for this disintegration have been I do not pretend to know; a historian of morals might maintain that it represents a general, slowly developing fissuration of the main European tradition, which means, in the main, the Christian tradition. Social historians might need to go even further back. A historian of religions might want to go back to the ages of hero myths. Yeats, thinking in terms of folk life and the myth, was content to go no

farther back than the period between the death of Chaucer
and the birth of Shakespeare when, he held, life began to
break up into (rational) fragments. Others, disliking the
rule of kings, might trace the disintegration of traditional
certainties to the decline of English feudalism in the fifteenth
century. (The Battle of Bosworth Field, ending the Wars
of the Roses and establishing the Tudor monarchy, is every
schoolboy's date for the death of English feudalism.) A
Frenchman of like views, fortified by a dislike for the bourgeoisie, might settle for the seventeenth century and the
decline of the French aristocracy. Others might begin with
the French Revolution. There are those who blame everything on Darwin; others who blame (or praise) Freud; others
who concentrate on the idea that scientific knowledge in our
own generation has increased at such a rate that even scientific assurance has become loaded with wonder and all matter has become liquefied by speculation and skepticism. I
am relieved that such vast considerations are outside my
province. All I dare to observe is that there is this one unde-
niable difference between, say, Flaubert's Emma Bovary
and Sir Walter Scott's Diana Vernon — that if Diana is a
"heroine" it can only be by a violent extension of meaning
that we call Emma also a "heroine." Emma may be a Heroine
in the eyes of some readers, and I am acquainted with more
than one reader who does admire her to this degree, but
unless the mass of readers are of the same opinion it is clear
that the use of the term is, to say the least, debatable. Flaubert was only fourteen years dead when the debate became
general in terms of the Dreyfus affair (1894-1906), which
showed that the term Hero was, all too clearly, an arguable
term. In our day the debate is universal. One of the saddest

modern instances of the enthronement and dethronement of
the Hero was Marshal Pétain. The dictators were base examples of the instability of the post. Contemporary Russia provides thousands of instances.

III

These essays are part of that debate. To illustrate it I have
taken a handful of modern novelists. If they are representative of their period and vocation it would seem that the men
and women of literary talent who came to their majorities
between 1920 and 1930 were no longer able to write or think
or live as socially integrated citizens, but, rather, as more
or less isolated receptivities. Finding that the social world
about them provided them with no satisfying pattern for
living, no sense of a satisfactory destination, they naturally
could not see in that social world's social hero a satisfying
symbol of the good life. They replaced him by what, for
want of a better word, we have at last come to call the anti-
Hero.

This personage is, as I have already shown, descended,
tortuously, from several of those French novelists I have
mentioned, though primarily, perhaps, from Stendhal —
which may be why Stendhal is today *the* novelist's novelist.
The anti-Hero is a much less tidy and comfortable concept
than the social Hero since — being deprived of social sanctions and definitions — he is always trying to define himself,
to find his own sanctions. He is always represented as groping, puzzled, cross, mocking, frustrated, isolated in his man-
ful or blundering attempts to establish his own personal,
suprasocial codes. (One of the clearest of recent avatars in

Britain was Kingsley Amis's *Lucky Jim.*) He is sometimes ridiculous through lack of perspicacity, accentuated by an attractive if foolhardy personal courage. Whether he is weak, brave, brainy or bewildered he is always out on his own. Which was why, in those fateful twenties, writers quite deliberately began, in Aldous Huxley's image — it occurs in his Introduction to the *Letters* of D. H. Lawrence, whom he sees as an example of the process — to dig out private caves, or air-raid shelters, of their own, and there started to compose private satires, laments, fantasies and myths in the effort to fill the vacuum left by the death of the social Hero with asocial rebels, martyrs, misfits, minor prophets, or, in short, with aberrants and anti-Heroes. The chief function of these creations was to express the idealistic dissatisfaction of the young with the values of the old and their fervent longing for a better pattern of living than they had inherited and for a more attractive destination than that to which their elders' pattern seemed likely to lead them.

This idealistic fervor of the twenties was not recognized at the time. Elderly gentlemen, as Mr. Noel Annan has said of Leslie Stephen, cannot understand that "affectation, mockery, frivolity and extravagance are ways in which young men can criticise life seriously." The young were regarded by their elders as feckless and irresponsible. The authors they admired were considered as peculiar if interesting aberrants from the procession of tradition — Remarque, Barbusse, Mrs. Woolf, Eliot, Gertrude Stein, Gide, Céline, Cocteau, the early Mann, the later Lawrence, the later Joyce. In those days Bloomsbury was a joke word, and only journalists loved the apparently anarchist doings of the fashionable or Bohemian young. And it must have been difficult for anybody to realize

that the real reason why young men wanted to live with
negresses, or develop tender homosexual attachments, or
conduct tense *ménages à trois,* or drink too much, or be sex-
ually promiscuous, or dig up Piccadilly at two o'clock in the
morning dressed in the costumes of Louis XIV — there is a
charming photograph of a group doing exactly this in Patrick
Balfour's reminiscences of the period, *Society Racket* — was
that they felt the urge of the most high-minded ideals of
personal sincerity and truthfulness to make some gestures of
defiance at the "hypocrisies" that had given them a world
unfit to live in. So far as I know, it was not until the nineteen
forties that criticism of the twenties began to catch up on
prejudice. The first complete study of the period that I have
found — *Virginia Woolf and Bloomsbury,* by Irma Ranta-
vaara — was published in Helsinki in 1953. It is of interest
that this study was undertaken with the aid of a Rockefeller
Grant; and that long before that Virginia Woolf was re-
spected, well known and carefully studied at the Sorbonne.
The twenties came into their own in Britain as a serious and
formative period rather later than elsewhere.

I suppose it is fair to say that everybody now recognizes
that it would be absurd to apply such terms as feckless or
irresponsible to a period that produced such writers as Mrs.
Woolf, Elizabeth Bowen, Aldous Huxley, Graham Greene,
Ernest Hemingway, William Faulkner or Evelyn Waugh —
the writers dealt with in this book — all of whom are nowadays taken seriously and, with one or two possible exceptions, better left unnamed, considered quite respectable. And
this is to make no mention of writers whom even the period
regarded as wholly traditional. Besides, to form a complete
literary image of the time, the generations must be allowed

to overlap. D. H. Lawrence, John Cowper Powys, Joyce, Yeats, Lytton Strachey, Somerset Maugham were all writing at the top of their form in the twenties. To leave these out because they were of an earlier generation would be to form a very squint-eyed picture of the decade. Furthermore, this overlapping of the generations is crucial for a reason apart altogether from literary figures; which is, that tradition can sturdily persist behind all appearances of outward change. This is particularly true of Britain, where influences can travel far and wide from sources unobserved at the time through a grapevine network impossible to map until revealed slowly, and sometimes long after, by the publication of memoirs, letters, biographies or even state papers. The twenties have not in this respect been mapped at all so far.

Consider, to take but one example, the light thrown on the period of the short essay called "My Early Beliefs" by the late Lord Keynes. It appeared posthumously in 1949, in the little book called *Two Memoirs*. It was a paper written originally for a private club in 1938. Keynes was recording, for private ears, an influence that had a profound effect on his set as far back as 1903. I will come to the nature of this influence in a moment. Here let us first note how it spread, and continued into the twenties. Note, first, the people who crop up in the memoir, all associates or old friends, sometimes referred to by Christian names or even pet names — Bertie for Earl Russell, Ludwig for Ludwig Wittgenstein, Bob Trevy for the poet R. C. Trevelyan, Bunny for David Garnett, Clive for Clive Bell, and so on. Note then how they interconnect. The first focus we observe is Cambridge. From Trinity College and King's: Bertrand Russell, R. C. Trevelyan, E. M. Forster, W. H. Macaulay, Desmond McCarthy. (The one Oxford man is Lord Robert Cecil, whose nephew Lord David Cecil was to marry McCarthy's daughter.) We observe next a familiar geographical and temperamental focus: that of Bloomsbury. Keynes was living at the time at 46 Gordon Square. Lady Ottoline Morell, formerly Lady Bentinck, half sister of the Duke of Portland, a great patroness, had married Philip Morell and was living at 10 Gower Street. Clive Bell was living at 50 Gordon Square. He married Vanessa Stephen, the daughter of Leslie Stephen and sister of Virginia Stephen, who married Leonard Woolf. The Woolfs were living at 52 Tavistock Square, where they ran the Hogarth Press. This links up with the publishing business and, through Leonard, with the whole *Nation,* later the *New Statesman,* set and many of the clever younger writers, such as Raymond Mortimer, Eddie Sackville-West, Stephen Spender, John Lehmann, Christopher Isherwood and William Plomer. When David Garnett joins forces with Francis Birrell to run a bookshop just behind Shaftesbury Avenue, we observe another link with such publishers as Fisher Unwin and Jonathan Cape and another batch of young writers through David's father Edward, one of the most influential publisher's readers of his time. We hear of others who foregathered in this set: Mark Gertler the painter, Roger Fry, Lytton Strachey, Goldsworthy Lowes Dickinson, Duncan Grant; several Cambridge dons, such as Sir Walter Durnford, Provost of King's College from 1918 to 1926; G. E. Moore, professor of philosophy, the McTaggart lecturer in moral sciences at Trinity from 1897 to 1923; and J. T. Sheppard, Provost of King's College after Durnford.

Next, if one were to trace the radiations from each of these through friends and professional connections one would evidently begin to get a wide-spreading map of unobtrusive but powerful influences in contemporary English thought. So, as one reads Virginia Woolf's *A Writer's Diary*, other names come in: Elizabeth Bowen, Rose Macaulay, Roger Senhouse, whose name links us with another publishing house, that of Secker and Warburg; Gerald Duckworth, another publisher, who was half brother to Virginia Woolf; Dorothy Wellesley, the poet, wife of Lord Gerald Wellesley, and later an intimate friend of Yeats; Anthony Asquith.*

Now, of all these names, Lord Keynes was mainly concerned in his memoir with one man and one book: the *Principia Ethica* of G. E. Moore. Moore's book was published as far back as 1903. Its influence was profound. "The habits of feeling," Keynes wrote of its influence, "formed then still persist in a recognisable degree. It is those habits of feeling influencing the majority of us which makes this Club a collectivity and separates us from the rest. X . . . We never lost a resilience the younger generation never seems to have had. They have enjoyed at most only a pale reflection of something not altogether superseded, but faded and without illusions." (This "faded and without illusions" may suggest at once both his own inadequacy to pass on a message of great value and the cooler mood of the thirties listening with respect but with less hope to their elders.) But when we see what was taught by this "Sacred Book" of Moore's, as it has been called by Mr. Noel Annan, we see that something of its message must nevertheless have seeped through.

It may be that the still popular phrase "state of mind"

---

* I am here much indebted to a Third Programme talk by Mr. Noel Annan on "The Mood of the Twenties," printed in the *Listener*, February 8, 1951. Mr. Annan's biography of Leslie Stephen is also suggestive. On Mrs. Woolf's death, appreciations in *Horizon* intimately evoked the original Bloomsbury.

("My dear, I found him in *such* a state of mind!") originated
with Moore. For the core of the Moore position was that
(quoting Keynes) "nothing mattered except states of mind
. . . not associated with action or achievement. . . . They
consisted in timeless, passionate states of contemplation and
communion, largely unattached to 'before' and 'after.'" I
think anybody reading the novels of the twenties might well
have occasion to revert constantly to these two things: the
divorce from *achievement;* and the consequential detachment *in time* from "before" and "after." (It would be amusing to think that we could link up, say, Graham Greene's
or Ernest Hemingway's concept of time as "screened at both
ends" with the *Principia Ethica* of Cambridge rationalism.)
The appropriate subjects of contemplation, while in these
timeless states of mind, were a beloved person, beauty and
truth; and the prime objects in life were held to be love, "the
creation and enjoyment of aesthetic experience and the pursuit of knowledge." It was not, however, a hedonist philosophy. It was an Epicurean philosophy. Its disciples thought
themselves rationalists to begin with, discovered only when
they had been involved that they were neo-Platonists, and
were ultimately to confess, as Keynes did, that their religion
within this philosophy closely followed the English Puritan
tradition of being chiefly concerned with the salvation of
their own souls. Pleasure was sternly decried, though as the
world drew them out, it had to be admitted that the neo-
Platonic contemplation of physical female beauty did tend
to the carnal enjoyment thereof, and that as the first rapture
wore away, there entered into the lives of the disciples of
idealism what the language of the period described as hot
intrigues. But, at first, they were so serious about everything

that when Keynes and Sheppard maintained one night that there was nothing wrong in itself about being cheerful, they at once fell into deep disgrace in their set.

Now, the cardinal point in all this is the reference to personal salvation. For, essentially, this ethic of Moore's is a thoroughgoing defense of individualism, and as such must have entirely pleased the individualistic twenties. If, however, we see that the effect was to draw people away from the older, Victorian, social-minded ethic, which saw man as a servant of his society, as undoubtedly happened, this was not entirely Moore's fault.

It is true that Moore argues that it is a logical error to suppose that the good can be defined as whatever gives the greatest happiness to the greatest number; that the good is distinct, to be appreciated by personal intuition, enjoyed and contemplated when one is in a good state of mind; but he did consider rules of conduct. However, Keynes records:

> We set on one side not only that part of Moore's fifth chapter on "Ethics in Relation to Conduct" which dealt with the obligations so to act as to produce by causal connection the most probable maximum of eventual good through the whole procession of future ages, but also that part which described the duty of the individual to obey general rules. We entirely repudiated a personal liability on us to obey general rules. We claimed the right to judge every individual case on its merits, and the wisdom, experience and self-control to do so successfully. This was a very important part of our faith and for the outer world our most important and dangerous characteristic. We repudiated entirely customary morals, traditions and traditional wisdom. We were, that is to say, in the strict sense of the term immoralists.

The stress, then, is on personal sincerity. Its source lies in the optimism of the first decade of the century, "the undisturbed individualism of those Edwardian days." When the second decade was broken by the war of 1914, and the third decade was darkened by the disillusion of 1918 and after, the need for personal sincerity became not less but more urgent. It was to become the hallmark of the decade of disillusion never again to hope except in total honesty.

The irony of it was that the sincerity of those Epicurean forerunners did not, in fact, appeal at all, in the form of its original definition, to the young people who came of age in the twenties. It was too withdrawn, too hothouse; perhaps they would have said it was smug. Even Keynes had come to see that there was some truth in this attitude, as he admits in his last paragraph referring to that writer who was very close to the heart of the twenties, D. H. Lawrence:

> And if I imagine us as coming under the observation of Lawrence's ignorant, jealous, irritable, hostile eyes, what a combination of qualities we offered to arouse his passionate distaste: this thin rationalism skipping on the crust of the lava, ignoring both the reality and the value of the vulgar passions, joined to libertinism and comprehensive irreverence . . . a regular skin-poison. All this was very unfair to poor, silly, well-meaning us. But . . . there may have been just a grain of truth when Lawrence said, in 1914, that we were "done for."

The ungrateful young people of the twenties were to agree in general with Lawrence's "done for"; and in agreeing they were to lump all their elders together, indiscriminately. It is only now, when they are themselves in their fifties, that they are able to discriminate calmly between elders and elders,

and to realize how far some of these elders were their cred-
itors. The reason they did not see and acknowledge it earlier
is that there was a split in their ranks around the early
thirties when the Pylon Poets appeared, hailing the coming
social revolution, finding their inspiration in machinery and
the masses, basing their attitude to life on the need for being
thoroughly social-minded. Then came the Spanish Civil War,
and then the Second World War, when for a period Russia
was the darling of the social-minded Left. The socialist triumph in Britain after the war and the utter cynicism of the
Russians' political technique shook these apples off every
tree. Before 1950 there was already hardly a writer left in
Britain who any longer thought it essential to be social-
minded. Moreover, there had been such a hullabaloo of
admiration for "the people" during the war that everybody
became sick to death of them. The upshot of it all is that
the term "antisocial" no longer now has the awful meaning
of a selfish insistence on individual liberty harmful to society.
If anything, "antisocial" means the opposite — a selfish insistence by the greedy masses on their rights, harmful to individual liberty. Mr. Noel Annan has drawn attention to the
fact that this is the wheel coming full circle; for, away back
in the Epicurean heyday, this was precisely how "antisocial"
was defined by Bertrand Russell: as the equation of anti-
individualist. It was the natural Epicurean attitude, and it
was the natural attitude of all the young people after the
First World War.

From what other attitude could have come all those (so
often boring and whining) novels about young men with
obtuse fathers, young men who had been bullied at school,
young men hopelessly misunderstood in dull bourgeois

homes? Indeed, it was then that the word bourgeois first
began to take on a pejorative sense, but for reasons of sensibility and not for political reasons. The Pylon Poets twisted
it to their own uses, never thinking what types had first
dethroned it. The word has, alas, never been rehabilitated.
There was a snobbery about poverty after the twenties. Men
like Sean O'Casey became lords of poverty, and men like
Mr. John Betjeman had to arrive before anybody born with
even an electroplated spoon in his mouth ceased to cringe
at the charge of having been born of respectable or well-off
parents. But the bourgeois virtues, and they are many, have
not appealed to writers since then. Mr. Waugh, born of that
sound stock, sold his inheritance for the aristocracy, the
Catholic Church and the British Army. His contemporaries
sold their inheritance for nothing at all.

Not, to be sure, that Bloomsbury was the whole of the
twenties, even of the literary twenties. It had no direct influence, for example, on Waugh, though I find it hard to believe
that he could have been entirely unaware of it. (Was anybody at the time entirely unaware of it?) He would, at least,
without knowing very much about it — he admits that he
never heard of G. E. Moore — have scorned it, been one of
those who thought it too hothouse, too withdrawn, too afraid
of the wide world. One reason why he would not have been
influenced, at least through personal contact, by the sort of
people Keynes mentions is that he was not a Cambridge
man. Of the Bloomsbury set (so far as I know) only Raymond Mortimer and Cyril Connolly did not come from the
younger university, and Connolly was never trusted by
Bloomsbury. This is the significance of the reference in Mrs.
Woolf's *Diary* to "those trusty Cambridge chaps." Unlike

"the Grigs" (meaning Mr. Geoffrey Grigson), they could
always be expected to sympathize with her work. Indeed,
they encouraged her loyally and effectively, if, also, far too
uncritically. Waugh belonged to a much gayer set, a sort of
High Bohemia, centered around Lady Cunard, Lord Berners
and the Sitwells, a blend of the more eccentric aristocracy
and the more amusing artists who destroyed the old-fash-
ioned Low Bohemia of Augustus John. The sort of people
who visited Lord Berners at Farringdon were certainly very
different from the intellectuals who drank cocoa and talked
late into the night at Gordon Square. They included such
people as all "the Mitford girls," "the Lygon girls" (Lord
Beauchamp's daughters), John Betjeman, Lady (Dolly)
Castlerosse, Phyllis de Janzé — she ran a fashionable hat-
shop in Bond Street — Lettice ("Duchess") Ashley-Cooper,
Patrick Balfour. Of Lord Berners one is told that, not caring
for the color scheme of his fields, he had his cows painted
blue. Apocryphal or not, the story suggests that although
he also had a town house where the Oxford-Cambridge paths
must sometimes have crossed, one cannot make too much of
the fact. The two sets could also have crossed paths at Rosa
Lewis's pub in Jermyn Street after the races, and it is
unlikely that any of the guests spent much time there discussing the true, the beautiful and the good. Nevertheless,
though the gay and the serious may not have mingled frequently or intimately, and though the Mitford Girls, or the
Lygon Girls, or Mr. Waugh may not have spent much of
their wild youth in reading, they must occasionally have
read something. By the time Waugh was writing his first
book, Mrs. Woolf had published nine books, Eliot four, and
E. M. Forster had completed his canon. It is inconceivable

that such books were not known to High Bohemia. However, I have no wish to suggest to any living relic of High Bohemia that he or she sometimes stole away quietly from the champagne bucket to the cocoa samovar to practice high thinking in secret in a Bloomsbury flatlet. All one may fairly stress is that when we read the novels of Waugh, or even of Miss Mitford, as when we read the poetry of John Betjeman, we must often not only feel the old acedia, the old sadness, the old seriousness breaking through the superficial lightheartedness but feel that it is this undertone which gives to their work whatever lasting value time will accord to it. It is of interest, in passing, to note one great difference between these Bohemians of the twenties and their modern counterparts, as seen in the plays of, say, Mr. John Osborne (*Look Back in Anger*): the twenties were represented mainly by the upper classes.

They were all sad young men, but they had great courage; after all, they looked coldly enough at life, and then had the courage to handle its unattractive, apparently unmalleable material, to create, to give birth in days of famine. They may have been a generation astray, but they were not in the least a lost generation. They made literature out of loss — Huxley has been doing it all his life; so did Scott Fitzgerald. They wrote and composed under a sense of doom, beating time. It is the feeling one always gets from Gershwin's *Rhapsody in Blue:* that opening sky-rocketing, dismayed wail of the clarinet, the frightening, mocking meowings of the saxophone, the hurrying speed as of men hurrying to get their song finished before the train crashes, the pianist dropping nervously the premonitory rains of the coming thunderstorm, the famous central melancholy melody that might well be the

decade's Hymn to Sorrow, its elegy for The Good Time Our
Fathers Lost Us. Sad, yes, but only because they wanted so
much that life should be worthy of their dreams, laughing,
even as they thought of it, with twisted mouths, suffused by a
desperate frenzy to unfurl a flag. It was equally in keeping
that Waugh should have become a commando in the Second
World War, and that Huxley should have retired to the
desert and mysticism, a marooned pirate throwing out endless bottles of invective from his sandy shore. It was anything
but a disheartening period. A period that laid the greatest
possible strain on the individual soul produced some of the
strongest personal assertions in our time. If affirmations were
beyond them that was not their fault. Nobody can affirm out
of personal integrity alone. Only when certainty returns to
men at large, that is, to what we call the world, can affirmation return to literature, and with it the representative Hero.
And that, surely, depends on the re-emergence for the purposes of the arts of a general body of human faith. (A large
subject on which I have inadequately touched in my final
essay.) Nobody wants affirmation for affirmation's sake. It
depends on what is affirmed. As well as Barbarossa there are
the barbarians. Sometime in the twenties a cartoon in *Sim-
plicissimus* mentioned this dilemma by depicting Barbarossa
leaning asleep over his table, his beard growing down
through the slab, while on the ground beneath, also awaiting
in his sleep the trumpet call of the resurrection, lay Kaiser
Wilhelm, his pointed mustaches horning up through the
hero's table. It is an inelegant problem on which even now,
perhaps more than ever now, it is impossible to make any
elegant comment. Since we became aware of it we have all
been stumbling. One recurs to the thought that the wonder

of the twenties was not so much that they wrote so well but that they wrote at all. Perhaps their secret recipe was to make themselves our scapegoats. The novelist, unable to establish any happy equilibrium between his personality and his milieu, sacrificed himself and his characters, the two imaginatively one, for our sake. Whether a Christian or not, he relived the Christian myth, with the vast difference that his martyrdom was entirely gratuitous in that he redeemed nobody but himself. It seems a better way of seeing modern literature than when Mlle. Claude Edmonde Magny suggests that Faulkner exorcises his agony by brushing it off on the reader. The truth seems to be, rather, that Faulkner dies in agony all over again every time he writes a novel. Or perhaps Camus is more to the essential point when he says, in *L'Homme Revolté,* that "the individualist cannot accept history as it is: he must destroy reality, not collaborate with it, in order to affirm his own existence." Which implies an utter revolt that has forced the conceptual Hero to give way to a new central type, whether Spartacus or Sebastian, the tortured Martyr.

The Vanishing Hero

HUXLEY and WAUGH

I do not think, therefore I am

ONE of the more fascinating and tantalizing problems that face the reader of fiction is to see how, and how far, a novelist can or does convey his own attitude to life through characters for whose views it would be impertinent to hold him responsible, and for whose behavior he can, at most, be held only partly responsible. It is a major problem for the reader of the novels of Aldous Huxley, since so many of his characters are continually uttering opinions on all sorts of subjects, and since so many of them are so unattractive that the general picture of the life they lead is, though described with wit and intelligence, more than depressing. Do those novels surreptitiously reflect Mr. Huxley's view of life at the time he wrote them, or was he an entirely neutral reporter dissociating himself utterly from what he reported?

Are those novels faithful documentaries, or are they personal parables?

Since I not only read them as entertaining personal parables but regard all novels, other than novels of pure pastime, as entertaining personal parables, it will be well for me to define a novel forthwith. A novel is a narrative, dealing with a number of characters whom the author has succeeded in making interesting and persuasive, and whom he deploys in a manner which, with his personal view of life, he considers fitting, and we with him. The fate, the views, the passions, the follies, the prejudices which he bestows on his characters imply his unspoken comment on life in general. For he does not need at any time to give explicit utterance to any comment; he will hope, rather, to elicit some comment from the reader; and if he elicits from us what he considers the correct comment he has succeeded in writing a persuasive novel. He has also, so to speak, given himself away, since our comment is his, inserted into our minds by suggestion under the hypnosis of the dramatic spectacle he has invented. Even his selection of certain types, out of all possible types, must be taken as intimating some such intention on his part; and when, as Huxley did in those novels of the twenties, he repeats himself in this way, he must be emphasizing his intention. It is for us to free ourselves from his hypnotic suggestion, to open our minds to the pattern he is emphasizing, to consider it by the light of our own experience or imaginative sympathy, to agree with its relevance to actual life or to disagree with it. This is why, incidentally and relevantly, there is, properly speaking, no such thing as historical fiction, since history lays obvious limitations on a writer's personal choice of types and above all on his autonomy in deploying them towards what he, with his view of life, considers their fitting behavior and fate. What I am saying is really an old thing: that every creative writer is to a large degree writing himself and that there is, ultimately, no such state of mind for a creative writer as total detachment.

Huxley has always shown a good deal of skill in giving us the illusion that he is quite detached or neutral. It is, however, almost entirely the illusion of one form of detachment, that which the intelligent writer may achieve — or seem to achieve — by the practice of intellectual discipline. Unfortunately for himself as a novelist he has practically nothing of that power — which Joyce, for instance, possessed in abundance, and which is essential to the truly effective novelist — whereby a writer associates himself sympathetically (or, if one prefers, empathically) with his characters in all their feelings, while skillfully concealing the fact from us. His intellect works too hard for that. His human sympathy is limited. His persuasiveness is of the order of a witty radio commentator announcing plausibly, "Now Gumbril is saying . . . Mrs. Aldwinkle is now entering the room and . . . Mr. Quarles thinks that . . ." We concentrate on the momentary saying, doing and thinking; the characters in their roundness — not that they have any roundness — easily disappear from our minds; we really scarcely see them at all; it is like a film in which only the sound track is working and the screen is blank; we are chiefly conscious of the skill of the script-writer. At that point the illusion of intellectual detachment breaks down, since we realize that the whole comedy has been manipulated by the author for his own purposes. With a true novelist, actually detached or not, we believe that the characters are autonomously alive and by this livingness they make us forget the author. The result is that when we recall the novels of Mr. Huxley we never talk much about the characters but a great deal about Mr. Huxley and his ideas.

This does not mean, however, that the ideas of his characters are his ideas. For example:

> They sat a long time over their cigarettes; it was half past three before Mrs. Viveash suggested they should go.
> "Almost time," she said, looking at her watch, "to have tea. One damned meal after another. And never anything new to eat. And every year one gets bored with another of the old things. Lobster, for instance, how I used to adore lobster once! But today — well, really, it was only your conversation, Theodore, that made it tolerable."
> Gumbril put his hand to his heart and bowed. He felt suddenly extremely depressed.
> "And wine: I used to think Orvieto so heavenly. But this spring, when I was in Italy, it was just a bad muddy sort of Vouvray. And those soft caramels they call Fiats; I used to eat those till I was sick. I was at the sick stage before I'd finished one of them, this time in Rome." Mrs. Viveash shook her head. "Disillusion after disillusion."

Huxley does not here say that life is disillusion after disillusion. It is Mrs. Viveash who says it. Nevertheless, the general tone and effect of the passage is so often repeated in those first four novels that we become sensitive to the emphasis and seek for the purpose of it. When this theme of the disillusioning effect of a surfeit of pleasure recurs and recurs, when so many characters are made to chase pleasure and find it so often dust and ashes, we are driven to think that Huxley is, in effect, saying that, for such people as he so frequently depicts, all pleasure, and, it may be, all happiness, is an illusion. The question straightway arises in our minds: Are these types abnormal, does he consider them abnormal and are we expected to think of them as abnormal? It would appear from the epigraph which he selected for *Point Counterpoint* that he considers them types of all humanity:

Oh, wearisome condition of humanity,
Born under one law, to another bound,
Vainly begot and yet forbidden vanity,
Created sick, commanded to be sound.
What meaneth nature by these diverse laws,
Passion and reason, self-division's cause?

Abnormal they may be to us; they are to him parables of the normal problem of mankind, though not necessarily of mankind's normal handling of the diverse laws of nature. This parabolic treatment permits Huxley to present us with a set of somewhat fantastic characters, even eccentrics, and extravagant situations without arousing our protest or disbelief — disbelief never even arises, nor belief either: such as the baron or the scientist in *After Many a Summer* and the whole idea of recessive rejuvenation. It is not the characters we are intended to accept, or not more than is necessary to sustain a mild interest and qualified assent; it is the moral to which their behavior points, and some — it is impossible to say which — of the ideas they propound.

For the multitude of brilliant and amusing ideas in which these novels abound cannot be ignored as part, even though what part nobody can say, of the general parable. Indeed, the trouble with them is that they tend to swamp the novels as novels, a fact which Huxley was probably admitting

through the Notebook of Philip Quarles in *Point Counterpoint,* in such passages as:

> Novel of ideas. The character of each person must be im-
> plied, as far as possible, in the ideas of which he is the
> mouthpiece. In so far as theories are rationalisations of senti-
> ments, instincts, dispositions of soul, this is feasible. The
> chief defect of the novel of ideas is that you must write
> about people who have ideas to express — which excludes all
> but about .01 of the human race. Hence the real, the con-
> genital novelists don't write such books. But then I never
> pretended to be a congenital novelist.

And again:

> The great defect of the novel of ideas is that it's a made-
> up affair. Necessarily; for people who can reel off neatly-
> formulated notions aren't quite real; they're slightly mon-
> strous. Living with monsters becomes tiresome in the long
> run.

These, then, are novels of ideas which are the rationaliza-
tions (to use Philip Quarles's words) of certain sentiments,
instincts, dispositions of soul in a number of characters selected to convey the author's life view and to point his moral.

I use the word *moral* uncomfortably. It is too explicit to
indicate the general impression with which we are left. Yet
some such word seems necessary to indicate that Huxley
gives us throughout the strongest feeling that he has been
trying to leave us with more than a vague, general impression. The critical quality of his approach, the highly intelligent mind that he displays, the ostensibly neutral or detached attitude of the stratospheric intellectual surveying the
follies of mankind seem to promise a general conclusion, or

set of conclusions, which is a much more pointed thing than a general impression. The "congenital" novelist is content with drawing a wash of feeling, like a wash of color, over the landscape of life; he communicates his instinctive feelings rather than his logical certainties. One, rightly or wrongly, expects more, being led to expect more, from the novelist of ideas.

But the deeper source of my discomfort in using the word *moral* in this context is the sense of disappointed expectation that attaches to it, and which, if valid generally — if, that is, it is not merely a personal expectation which others do not also feel — points to Huxley's central problem and weakness as a novelist. For the general conclusion, or moral, or practical lesson, or general principle of the author's thought or life view does not in the end emerge with anything like the clarity one expects from a man of such apparently superlative intelligence. All one can do is to induce it confusedly and unsatisfactorily from the underlying spirit of invective, which one feels to be just as instinctive and emotional as in any congenital novelist. One is finally driven to conclude that all Huxley's intellectual paraphernalia conceals an intelligence at war with itself, or struggling vainly for a clear position from which to attack. And while in this essay I am interested directly only in the early novels, it would be unrealistic not to bear in mind also the constant gropings and changes of position in his later work.

The result has been that he has from the beginning attempted satire and achieved only what I have called invective. The absence of a firm standpoint made this inevitable, since of its nature satire implies a clear standpoint, or acceptable norm, from which to castigate those who would deny, insult or attempt to overthrow it. Breughel's pictures of country boors at play are in this sense aristocratic pictures, and imply not his judgments alone but those of his society. Pope's satires are the judgments of a devoted, even fanatical Tory driven to despair of his country by the triumph of the Whigs. That the standpoint of either may be absurd or perverse does not arise, except in final judgments of the universality and permanence of their ideas, whereupon one may elevate Boileau or Pascal above Pope or Breughel. If satire were not firmly based in this way on some widely accepted norm it might well be considered an impertinence on the part of any man to put himself into the judgment seat; wherefore it has been well said of Pope, by Mark Pattison, that it was well for him that his personal spite, pettiness, meanness, ungenerosity and vanities were balanced by his debt to the universal spirit of his age. It was Huxley's misfortune as a would-be satirist to have been born into an age in which the writer found himself a rebel against all tradition. His great interest for us, as it must be for subsequent generations, lies in his being such a perfect representative of an angry and disoriented decade gallantly exploring a sea of doubt; though it would be unjust and incomplete to regard him merely as the castigator of one peculiar, or abnormal, set of people: these are the means, or metaphors, by which he expresses the perplexities inherited by his decade as a whole from what it considered its unworthy ancestry.

What a living image he presents to us of that era, at once bored and perplexed, disillusioned and unhappy, bewildered and groping, lost and seeking for firm land, now excited, now hopeful, now overcome by despair! He conveys it

for the most part by juxtaposition, by point and counterpoint. So, in *Those Barren Leaves:*

> "I don't see that it would be possible to live in a more ex-
> citing age," said Calamy. "The sense that everything's per-
> fectly provisional and temporary — everything, from social
> institutions to what we've hitherto regarded as the most sa-
> cred scientific truths — the feeling that nothing, from the
> Treaty of Versailles to the rationally explicable universe, is
> really safe, the intimate conviction that anything may hap-
> pen, anything may be discovered — another war, the artifi-
> cial creation of life, the proof of continued existence after
> death — why, it is all infinitely exhilarating."
> "And the possibility that everything may be destroyed?"
> questioned Mr. Cardan.
> "That's exhilarating too," Calamy answered, smiling.
> "It may be rather tame of me," Mr. Cardan said, "but I
> confess, I prefer a more quiet life. I persist that you made a
> mistake in so timing your entry into the world that the pe-
> riod of your youth coincided with the war and your early
> maturity with this horribly insecure and unprosperous
> peace . . ."

And he proceeds to contrast his own youth, spent in calm
faith in the placid bosom of nineteenth-century materialism.
It is a characteristic contrast between Calamy, the sincere if
weak romantic who will end up as a sort of mystic, and
Cardan, the self-avowed practical man and almost total
skeptic who impresses himself as something of a sponger. A
few pages on, the counterpoint is repeated on the terrace of
Mrs. Aldwinkle's house when that lady, who has believed
too long "in passion, passionately," feels that the starry
nights of Italy explain the passion of the south, and Calamy
agrees, but Cardan twists it all around to the climate, the

effect of heat on inducing idleness, the ample leisure that
accompanies idleness and the evident conclusion that "passion can only flourish among the well-fed unemployed." It is
a typical Huxleyan sequence, written in a technique of non-
committal irony which is much more near to the irresponsibility of Restoration comedy than the didactic comedy of
Shaw. The ideas are adumbrated with a skeptical smile —
and left unresolved. Yet they *are* adumbrated, in the form
either of difficult, if not unanswerable, questions or of opposing theories, sometimes explicitly stated by their own
type-characters, but not always stated, sometimes merely indicated by their behavior, their dilemmas, the predicaments
into which they get themselves by having been all too true
to type.

Those Barren Leaves is one of the most readable, representative, effective and clear of Huxley's novels. It will show
us more easily than any other of his novels how he proceeds.
The novel is placed chiefly in Italy, with flashbacks to England. Somewhere in the Apuan hills, near Spezia, a sagging
huntress of social and literary lions named Lilian Aldwinkle
has bought a Malaspina palace, wherein she collects a number of guests. The device is a simple one — a cruising liner,
an island, an inn cut off by the snow, a long-distance bus;
they have often been used for this purpose by novelists who
want either dramatic action or psychological analysis. Huxley is not interested in either; he chiefly wants to set his people talking. He does stoop to a few elementary events or
episodes, but, as in the Aristotelian *Poetics,* these are not
much more than a break or rift in the choric songs which
give us the main continuity. The main characters, besides
Mrs. Aldwinkle herself, are her pretty niece Irene; Miss

Thriplow, a Chelsea-ish novelist; a self-indulgent, fruity, obscurely gifted professional week-ender named Cardan; Mr. Falx, a Labor leader; Lord Hovenden, immensely rich, a Guild Socialist, under the influence of Falx; and Calamy, an intelligent, serious-minded bachelor who shares the role of central character with one Francis Chelifer, a cynical, self-disbelieving dilettante who composes occasional poems and witty aphorisms when not editing, in Gog's Court, Fetter Lane, the *Rabbit Fancier's Gazette,* with which is incorporated the *Mouse Breeder's Record.* He is not well off; he lives in a Chelsea boardinghouse. Mrs. Aldwinkle literally picked him up off the beach after he had been all but drowned. His mother, Mrs. Chelifer, also appears, and a dotty creature named Miss Elver, whose brother has brought her to Italy in the feeble-minded hope that she will die of malaria and that he will inherit her fortune.

It emerges that Miss Thriplow is a self-conscious woman who has so corroded her natural emotions by constantly dramatizing them that it would not be unjust to describe her as almost completely bogus. That the serious-minded Calamy should casually bed with her is clearly intended not as a tribute to her charms but to the frailty of his intelligence and his will, and since he ultimately retires to a peasant's hut to ponder upon the inmost nature of reality, we cannot help feeling that we are intended to look back with grave apprehensions from the hardships of the peasant's pallet to the pleasures of the lady's bed. Cardan emerges as a pragmatist, a materialist, a self-called practical man, and we must conclude that we are to trace his boasted realism to a core of weak self-indulgence when we see him marrying the unfortunate lunatic, Miss Elver, for her money. Mrs. Aldwinkle decides that Chelifer is a Shelley barely saved from drowning, and in her foolish romanticism she shamelessly tries to make him her lover. She is represented pitilessly as an aging Juno chasing impossible young love. We discover in Chelifer a thoroughly disillusioned cynic. In this atmosphere Falx might well fear that the young girl Irene must end by being corrupted — he thinks of the palace as "a bad house" — but happily Hovenden falls in love with her and, we may believe, saves her from destruction. It is without regret that we note that Hovenden and Irene have no clever ideas to propound: indeed, the only occasion when Irene does propound a "clever" idea — that "contraception has made chastity superfluous" — is that on which Falx begins to foresee her ruin. But, then, they are both simple souls, somewhat reminiscent of Nina and Adam in *Vile Bodies,* and Huxley is not, one feels, greatly interested in simple souls.

Nor, to be honest, are we in this novel. Our interest is in the play of opposing ideas. Of these ideas the clearest exponents are Francis Chelifer, Calamy and Cardan. They represent three concepts of reality. To Chelifer reality is what it seems to ninety-nine out of every hundred human beings, and he maintains that nobody has any right to run away from those brutish minds which preponderate in the universe. Calamy disagrees. Such people, in his view as a seeker after ulterior reality, are "content with appearances," such as the Harrow Road and the Café de la Rotonde, "call them realities and proceed to abuse any one who takes an interest in what lies underneath these superficial symbols as a romantic imbecile." Reality, to Cardan, is the social system where the wise man steers his way cunningly between the tribalistic Babbitts, over whom Chelifer gloats masochistically, and the few hyperoptimists, like Calamy, who shelter from the more unpleasant aspects of human behavior by simply dismissing them as surface appearances. If we could fully respect any of these three men, or feel that any of them had made, or was likely to make, an honorable success of his life we might feel that Huxley was using them to lead us to his own general conclusion. As it is, we are presented with three ways of life none of which, evidently, persuades him, and we must feel that the mockery he turns on all three characters reflects his despair at the power of human intelligence, including his own, to answer the problem he poses. At this point in our reading we might begin to be doubly glad that the only two people, Hovenden and Irene, who come out of the novel with some hope of happiness have no intellectual views on the subject at all. Had they been permitted any, they too, one fears, would also have been eviscerated by the invective of Huxley's pervasive misanthropy.

But every novel contains at least one character who seems closer to the sympathies of the author than any other, and one is aware of an increase of heat and interest whenever he takes the stage. Here the temperature of our interest rises whenever Chelifer appears. Certainly the section called "Fragments from the Autobiography of Francis Chelifer" has more life in it than any other, especially Chapter Five, wherein Huxley has embedded an excellent short-story beginning: "Her name was Barbara Waters." Here, at least, the moral is quite clear. Indeed, it is stated with passion.

Through Barbara, we are told, Chelifer learned the difficult art of "exclusive concentration on the relevant," meaning "the human reality in the centre of the pointless landscape." Barbara was more than his charmer; she was his sym-

bol of "an intense and secret and utterable happiness." She
had haunted him when a boy by her mysterious beauty; he
meets her again during the war and is enraptured again to
find that "within its ambush her soul kept incessant holi-
day." He continues to idealize her; but now he who had "desired all beauty, all that exists of goodness and truth, sym-
bolised and incarnate in one face" begins to desire her as an
individual woman, and he both nourishes this natural desire
and fears the revelation of its satisfaction. One foresees the
result. He writes, in his autobiography, looking back sadly at
it:

> All this were it to happen to me now would seem per-
> fectly natural and normal. If I were to make love to a young
> woman I should know precisely what I was making love to.
> But that, in those days, was something I had still to learn.
> In Barbara's company I was learning it with a vengeance. I
> was learning that it is possible to be profoundly and slav-
> ishly in love with some one for whom one has no esteem,
> whom one does not like, whom one regards as a bad charac-
> ter and who, finally, not only makes one unhappy but bores
> one. And why not, I might now ask, why not? That things
> should be like this is probably the most natural thing in the
> world. But in those days I imagined that love ought always
> to be mixed up with affection and admiration, with worship
> and an intellectual rapture, as unflagging as that one experi-
> ences during the playing of a symphony. Sometimes, no
> doubt, love does get involved with some or all of those
> things; sometimes these things exist by themselves, apart
> from love. But one must be prepared to swallow one's love
> completely neat and unadulterated. It is a fiery, crude and
> somewhat poisonous draught.

It is a summary of what happens to almost every character
in Huxley's novels who "tries" love. It is an echo of Mrs.

Viveash's "disillusion after disillusion." Barbara's mysterious, unearthly beauty is the mask of a trollop in a state of almost constant heat. Because he has idealized her he suffers
agonies of unhappiness at the loss of his dream. "I was happy
at the thought that I should soon be kissing her; miserable
because that was not how I wanted to love my imaginary
Barbara; miserable too, when I secretly admitted to myself
the existence of the real Barbara, because I felt it an indig-
nity to be the slave of such a mistress." One thinks of Tony
Last in Waugh's *A Handful of Dust* — "A whole Gothic
world had come to grief" — when Chelifer says, "Reality
gave imagination the lie direct."

When all self-deception ends, he adds up the sum of his
tormenting experience and the answer is:

> And it is the truth that men are cruel and stupid and that
> they suffer themselves to be driven to destruction by shep-
> herds as stupid as themselves. I thought of my passion for
> universal justice, of my desire that all men should be free,
> leisured, educated, of my imaginations of a future earth
> peopled by human beings who should live according to rea-
> son. . . . And this war, I thought. Was there the slightest
> prospect that any good would come of it? The war to end
> war! The argument was forcible enough this time; it was
> backed up with a kick in the breech, the most terrific kick
> ever administered. But would it convince humanity more
> effectively than any other argument had ever done?

Then he thinks that, for all that, men are courageous,
kind, patient and self-sacrificing and do not mean to be bad;
on which the only comment he can make is, "Forgive them
for they know not what they do." He thinks of the few who
are intelligently aware, but decides that they are merely odd

exceptions, irrelevant to the fundamental reality that this world in which we live is stupid. They are more lies, like the ideal of love, or his own quondam belief in justice. The whole episode, within the context of Chelifer's melancholy autobiography, is a vivid picture of the disillusion of the twenties.

It is also a perfect example of what I have called Huxley's hypnosis. Ideas are inserted in our minds; we want eagerly to argue about them: to say, for instance, that Chelifer is an ass who thinks that reality gives the lie direct to imagination merely because his silly fantasy has given the lie direct to nature; or to point out that because a girl prefers to be the trollop that she is rather than the angel somebody chooses to think her is no reason for enlarging misanthropically on the world in general. That we may wish to argue so is a tribute to the author. We cannot, however, attribute total responsibility for Chelifer's ideas to Huxley, nor even go so far as to say that he has had no right to compose the sequence with feelings of compassion or pity for Chelifer. This is, in theory, Chelifer himself weeping over his own wounded heart. All we can legitimately say is that the author, aware of the foolishness of Chelifer, must before the novel ends deploy him in a fitting manner, give him the fate which, with his own life view, he considers appropriate for such folly. Does he do so? As we have seen, Chelifer's fate is that he cannot escape from the votes of the masses as to the nature of reality, and that their view of life bores and disgusts him. "One has no right," he says, "to ignore what for every ninety-nine out of every hundred human beings is reality — even though it mayn't actually be the real thing." He even says, "If you want to know what human life is you must be courageous and live as the majority of human beings actually do live. It's singularly revolting, I assure you." The only explicit comment Huxley makes on this, through one of his (ambiguous) mouthpieces, is to suggest to us that Chelifer is an inverted sentimentalist; one, that is, who instead of seeing everything in a rosy light gloats over horrors; but it may strike us as a more adequate judgment on Chelifer that his folly leads him in the end to the death of all pleasure, all joy in life. This acedia is Huxley's usual punishment for his characters. From the viewpoint of the twenties it is the most cruel of all punishments. They knew the misery of boredom all too well.

Whose the fault? Their own? Or the "wearisome condition of humanity"? Huxley, it seems to this reader, here plays the part of jesting Pilate. Everything he has written in this period is, like Mr. Mercaptan's "Loves of the Pachyderms," "all very witty and delicately savage," but as for general conclusions, one may seek for them — indeed, as I have intimated, one is somehow led to expect them — but after one has discovered that one is not going to get them one ceases to ask for them any longer. And how could they arise in any novel about a groping period by a man who was evidently groping himself? *The Slough of Despond:* wittily described in several volumes by One Who Knows.

Too much has been left out for conclusions to arise: chiefly such elementary matters as the knowledge of good and evil. These characters are all in a strange dilemma: they have eaten of the apple, but like those curious early Oriental Gnostics known as the Naassenes who sang hymns of praise to the serpent of transgression, the knowledge they have acquired has taught them nothing either about good or about evil. They have learned only about the results of certain kinds of behavior to which they give no moral names. And their ultimate reactions are, as it happens, very like those of the Gnostics, who wavered between the hatred of matter and the embrace of matter according to their temperaments. Inevitably they have no philosophy, and any novel about them must be without any central figure to represent any satisfactory system of thought, or indeed any satisfactory system of behavior. Being all rebels or martyrs — there is no hero — happiness can only come to them momentarily. As Mrs. Quarles says to Marjorie Carling with characteristic Huxleyan wit, "Happiness is like coke — something you get as a by-product in the process of making something else."

As parables, the novels are fair pictures of the twenties; or, if one prefers, fair caricatures. I am not at all sure that one is entitled to ask if they are fair pictures, or caricatures, of life in general, then or at any time, but if one does ask, then one must say that they certainly — one may be so downright — are not. They are too absolute. That characters cut to the bone to represent absolute positions lose the complexity of human nature one may not mind, since these are novels of ideas not of character; but it is fatal to the universal application of these parables that characters who lack the complexity of human nature must, perforce, also oversimplify the questions they are intended to project.

Why is it that we relished these novels when they first appeared more than we do today? (One does not speak of an uncritical relish at either time; one can be critical and enjoy all the more for that; but today the enjoyment is quite different in that it is now devoid of the quality of glee which distinguished it in those years.) I can here only give my own feelings; which seem, when I examine them, to close in on a point which I raised early on: Huxley's detachment. I find that I form reservations about it amounting to an uncomfortable fear that it inadequately conceals that form of self-pity precisely defined by the author when speaking of Chelifer's inverted sentimentality which makes him, in wishing that the world were other than it is, concentrate on its most unpleasant elements. This form of sentimentality might be described as the feelings of a man, part aesthete, part Puritan, looking into a distorting mirror of life with a groan and a grimace. And this excess of Augustinian sensibility induces further reservations with regard to Huxley's integrity at this period of his development.

If a writer chooses to stand on his head nobody can object provided he does not pretend that he is not standing on his head. If Huxley is without ambiguity setting out solely to entertain us (using the word on the highest level) his pose, posture or approach is largely his own affair, though we will, as a matter of course, take note of these things if for no other reason than to decide how seriously he wishes to be taken. It may seem, however, that there is a certain amount of double shuffle in these novels. The author is an entertainer, but he is also an intellectual in the dictionary's sense of "a member of a class or group professing, or supposed to possess, enlightened judgment and opinions with respect to public or political questions." That sentimental streak to which I refer has begun to vitiate for me Huxley's detachment, and so his integrity and, finally, his intelligence. These early novels, while they remain entertaining parables, now appear to have been based on a wholly personal view of life which I do not find sufficiently inclusive to call intelligent. The impression a rereading of these novels gives one today is of an arid and desiccated waste, bordering at many points on jungles of odorous despair, always blessedly watered by a constant dew of bitter wit and otherwise illuminated not by intelligence but by brilliant intellectual pyrotechnics.

It is possible to perceive several other reasons why this should be the effect of the passage of time. Two seem to be more plausible than others. For one thing, these novels were topical novels in the sense in which Shaw's plays were often topical plays, and with changing conditions the ideas lose much of their appeal. Nowadays Huxley is most topical when he is discussing not contemporary society but the past and the future, and one will agree that history and prophecy are realms in which the imagination is least liable to be given the lie by reality. With this goes the fact that the spirit of the twenties, which produced and once responded so gleefully to the novels, is gone or quite altered. It was natural then to be sorry for oneself, to express one's disgust with the wearisome condition of humanity either by being puritanical or the reckless opposite, one's disbelief in society by denying sin and misdoubting virtue, one's contempt for traditional solutions by posing abstract questions to which one knew there was no real answer, to take refuge from the world in aestheticism, to show one's distrust of all large political conclusions by finding the hero type only in the lone wolf — D. H. and T. E. Lawrence were the ideal hero types of the era — because honesty and idealism could have no validity except for the individual or the very few. The uplifted right arms of the three dictators put an end to all that. Today we huddle, and listen uncomfortably to the not too hopeful prophets. But, leaving the times out of it altogether, how could they be hopeful? They never had been. Orwell, Koestler, Eliot, Huxley . . . One closes one's eyes at the thought that one of these days Mr. Graham Greene may decide to announce the future of the race.

Waugh's detachment, while having its own shape of ambiguity, is much more genuine than Huxley's. He is detached by hardness of mind, hardness of thought about people — not about affairs, or ideas, for he is not in any sense an intellectual; he is, or rather was in his great satirical period, a man of fashion with Joyce's trick of suddenly leaving the company to take satirical notes on his cuff in the washroom. Where this toughness springs from God (quite literally) alone knows: it was one of those inexplicable natural gifts like genius or personality. A biographer might find influences. One can now only guess at some of the things that helped detachment.

It must have helped that he early became a Roman Catholic. (Many critics who do not warm to the Catholic feeling in *Brideshead Revisited* seem to forget that Waugh had become converted to Catholicism in the year of the publication of his second novel.) For to be a Catholic in England is to be removed by many degrees from the main English tradition. Waugh himself wrote:

> The aesthetic appeal of the Church of England is unique and peculiar to these islands. . . . In England the . . . mediaeval cathedrals and churches, the rich ceremonies that surround the monarch, the historic titles of Canterbury and York, the social organization of the country parishes, the traditional culture of Oxford and Cambridge, the liturgy composed in the hey-day of English prose-style — all these are

the property of the Church of England, while Catholics meet in modern buildings, often of deplorable design, and are usually served by simple Irish missionaries.

Does one imagine a note of nostalgia, which would imply attachment-detachment, and promise sympathy and understanding? I cannot help recalling Newman after his conversion saying sadly to a fellow convert that his new friends had never known the world in which he, in memory, lives.

Then there is the class difference. A critic once described Waugh as a snob and he replied, "I think perhaps he is right in calling me a snob; that is to say, I am happiest in the company of the European upper classes." Happy, but possibly also all the more objective about them by not having been born into them. His grandfather was a country doctor from Somerset; his father, after Sherborne and New College, became a reader for Kegan Paul, later chairman of Chapman and Hall, a prolific critic and editor of the English classics. It is, in the sense in which one could apply the word to wealthy French families such as those of Laniel or Mendès-France, a bourgeois background. When Evelyn Waugh passed through Lancing and Hertford College he moved into a wider world, a step which it is not so easy to take in France as in England; unless one can equate the Jockey Club with St. James's and Buck's — Waugh's clubs — as open doors to the life of "the European upper classes"?

And there was his formative period, with its critical attitude to life in general and English life in particular. Had he been born fifteen years earlier or later he might have been led to join the Labor Party. (It may not sound likely; but one remembers that Wellington, Balliol and the Foreign Office could lead so skeptical a mind as the Hon. Harold Nicolson that way.) The kind of party that attracted Waugh's contemporaries led him to *Vile Bodies.*

> Masked parties. Savage parties. Victorian parties, Greek parties, Wild West parties, Russian parties, Circus parties, parties where one had to dress as somebody else, almost naked parties in Saint John's Wood, parties in flats and studios and houses and ships and hotels and night clubs, in windmills and swimming-baths, tea parties at school where one ate muffins and meringues and tinned-crab, parties at Oxford where one drank brown sherry and smoked Turkish cigarettes, dull dances in London and comic dances in Scotland and disgusting dances in Paris — all that succession and repetition of massed humanity. . . . Those vile bodies.

Even this brief run, culminating in the title of the novel, so characteristic of Waugh's style in its eclectic adjective, proposes a very different kind of mind to Huxley's, for though it inveighs, it does it with gusto, and one reads it not in admiring glee at the destruction wrought but with an amusement unalloyed by contempt for its victims. The adjective alone might put us at our ease, like a reliable name on an aircraft; we feel we are taking off with a good company in good company. *Vile* has no sour connotations. It is not depressing, it is not moral, it is young and lively and it is also old and reputable, a blend of Shakespeare and slang; it suggests a sort of hopeless, good-humored scorn of fate, chance or folly like a man who has gone for a long tramp in vile weather with a leaking mackintosh, and will describe his misfortunes afterwards with a blend of resignation and derision which does not exclude the suggestion that he enjoyed the adventure he reviles. Attachment-detachment again?

The effect of this genuine but ambiguous detachment of

Waugh's is that the laughter his first six novels evoke is our happy tribute to the delicate balance he strikes between his detachment from his characters which allows him to satirize them and his affection for them which allows him to pity them. Surely we all remember *Vile Bodies* as much for its compassion as its bite? Recall, for example, how generously he handles those two vile bodies Adam and Nina. They are a foolish young couple and he does not spare them the exposure of their folly, but he never suggests that they are wicked, and he does not moralize over them. They did anticipate their wedding night, but they loved one another truly; and as if to alleviate their unorthodox behavior Waugh so arranges things that Adam intended to anticipate lawful wedlock only by one night, and Nina yielded to him only because she was so touched by his silly dance of joy over the check he had extracted from her dotty father that she could not bear to point out to him that her papa had signed it with the name Charlie Chaplin. He grants them virtues, however foolishly applied, as when he allows them to visit the sick — Miss Runcible — though so boisterously that their kindness helps to polish her off. He does not spare them their choice of friends. Peter Pastmaster drinks like a fish and sleeps with negresses; Lady Metroland is a high-class procuress; Miles Malpractice is a homosexual; Mrs. Panrast is a Lesbian. But these are minor characters in the romance of Adam and Nina, and no society has ever been free of such aberrants. He makes Adam try to earn a living on which to marry Nina, though because he is an incompetent young fool he must be dogged by bad luck and always look like a silly young mug. Adam is entirely faithful to Nina and when he marries her we are to presume that they live happily ever after. Indeed, the unique thing about *Vile Bodies* is that this satire by an undeceived contemporary has achieved so much benevolence without an iota of sentimentality.

But, then, Waugh is sometimes charged with unnecessary cruelty towards his characters. Mr. Donat O'Donnell, for example, writes in his interesting study of a group of Catholic novelists, *Maria Cross:*

> Mr. Waugh is a great explorer of human disadvantages, and his unscrupulous adolescent cruelty in this is the common quality of his two most obvious characteristics: his humour and his snobbery. Two of his comic novels, *Black Mischief* and *Scoop,* are largely based on a sly appeal to the white man's sense of racial superiority; much of the best fun in *Decline and Fall* comes from the exploitation of Captain Grimes, who, although he claimed to be a public school man, was not really a gentleman and did not often have a bath; in *Put Out More Flags* the purest comedy lies in the lurid descriptions of the appearance and behaviour of three proletarian children.

One must agree that Waugh does, frequently, indulge in pointless cruelty, and that when he does so it is a mistake and a blemish. In *Black Mischief* Mr. Youkoumian treats his wife with such persistent and callous brutality that instead of laughing at her misfortunes we protest at them. But this is not usual with Waugh, and I think Mr. O'Donnell has here missed two points, one essential to an understanding of Waugh; and I can only hope that it may make him feel a little uncomfortable to recall that G. K. Chesterton, who thought that the disasters piled on the innocent head of the hero of *Decline and Fall* were merely "distressing," would be entirely on his side.

First: while it is true that the misfortunes of Mrs. Youkoumian are not funny, one must understand the analeptic mechanism of the sort of laughter they can produce. Some years ago a multiple murderer named John Christie was arrested, tried and hanged in London. He had enticed women into his flat, in the sort of quarter which would have been suitable for a Graham Greene or a Simenon crime story. He had strangled the women and stacked them up in a cupboard like coats on coat hangers, one in front of the other. Others he had buried. I have heard this case discussed not only by intellectuals but by ordinary, good-living, decent Irish people with peals of laughter. In Dublin he was commonly referred to as Corpus Christie. Before that a man named Haigh had melted down several women in barrels of acid so that nothing was left in the bottoms of the barrels but their false teeth. It was the only way by which one victim was identified. In the effort to escape the gallows Haigh not only pretended lunacy but declared that he drank his own urine. This also I have heard discussed with the utmost gaiety. Surely this sort of laughter is like a man who has drunk poison tickling his throat with a feather to make himself vomit the evil thing. Waugh is not, I feel, in his scenes of apparently gratuitous cruelty laughing at humanity, or laughing with humanity. His laughter is a horrible cathartic laughter. He invents a scapegoat who suffers the cruelty of life for us. We identify ourselves with the sufferer. We laugh it off. This does not make it funny. It does make it bearable. We have considered, faced up to cruelty and borne it by proxy in some form, to some degree.

Second: Waugh's cruelty is more often a deliberate, well-pointed and wholly admirable part of his technique, and if it is double-edged it is for sound reasons. This is where Mr. O'Donnell has not only missed a point but completely failed to understand what Waugh is generally driving at in his satires. True, the loathsome Mr. Basil Seal does make money during the war by packing dirty and destructive refugees into the gracious, well-loved, much-tended country homes of his neighbors, later withdrawing them for handsome bribes. But what is Waugh's purpose in this? Basil Seal is a type consistently despised by the twenties, a man without an iota of the admirable Epicurean private virtues they admired, and he is therefore clearly presented as a crook. On the other hand, the soft-headed, soft-boiled mugs whom he defrauded and tormented were largely the people who, by their soft-headed goodness, had brought all the trouble on the world in 1914; just as in the postwar decade they would be going around, still mugs, still soft-headed, asking people to sign peace pledges; just as later, in the thirties, these same people would be reading Auden, and Isherwood, and Spender, and Koestler and all the Pylon boys, who were the intellectual vanguard of the socialist revolution which would go far to wipe out the bourgeoisie completely — and would have done so if there were not in even the softest-headed British bourgeois some tough residue of the strain of Hampden and of Pym that not even the half-baked liberalism of the nineteenth century and the inhuman humanism of the first decades of the twentieth could wholly destroy. Waugh could not possibly have been on the side of these deluded souls, even against Seal. He regarded them much as a sergeant major might regard a thoroughly hopeless set of raw recruits; and he let them "have it."

Besides, the Basil Seals of the world had at least three

virtues in the eyes of the twenties; Basil Seal was clever, and amusing — "amusing" is still a popular word among English intellectuals, applicable to anything from Byzantine art to Boston baked beans — and he was not contributing to the complacency of the stupid good. He was therefore a useful Attila, a Scourge of God to lash the stupid good and carry off his wickedness in scornful laughter. It is almost always so in Waugh's novels. His hard-bitten scoundrels surpass his heroes and heroines: Basil Seal, Margot Beste-Chetwynde, who becomes Lady Metroland, Captain Grimes, Solomon Philbrick. Virtuous innocence is his laughingstock, personified by any of Seal's pathetic victims, or Paul Pennyfeather, or Adam Symes, or old Prendergast, or Cedric Lyne, or Tony Last, whose only fault was that he was a dull husband who did not know the ropes, and lived in an innocent (but to Waugh dangerous) dream of Gothic worlds with dappled unicorns on the lawn and childish toys sentimentally preserved in the bedroom cupboard — just the sort of fellow who would become a hero in a silly war like that just finished in 1918.

It is interesting to compare him in this with Marcel Aymé. One knows from *Le Confort Intellectuel* where Aymé's sympathies lie, but from his novels, if one did not know that whom the Lord loves He punishes, one might be puzzled to decide where his loyalties lie. They lie, one then sees, with that backbone of French life, as Aymé sees things, the bourgeois tradition, once solidly dependable, now become fuddled, corrupt, frightened, vain, and making an arrant fool of itself in its pursuit of all sorts of wrong ideas. This is why he lacerates the bourgeois family in *Travelingue;* their foolish, foppish gabble about the latest films, the nitwit daughters' disreputable guests, the father toiling, the mother squandering. It adds up to a moralist's picture with the same sort of effect as Waugh's savagery in sending the proletariat children of the London slums down into the half-timbered, lawn-shaven, brass-gleaming homes of the bewildered, well-meaning, fat-headed bourgeoisie of England. In *Le Chemin des Ecoliers,* likewise, Aymé piles misfortune on the heads of Michaud and Lolivier, good, honest, simple men, but so unwise, so sentimental, so unshrewd. (The novel is a revealing commentary on our notion of the agate-headed, tough-minded, calculating, vulpine French businessman.) Sentimentality is also the crime of Archambaud and Leopold in *Uranus;* they pay dearly for it, while the village boys literally get away with murder. But for the fifties as for the twenties the first commandment is: Thou shalt not be soft-headed or soft-hearted, because that way lies evil and death. Aymé, like Waugh, seems to be saying, challengingly, "Be clever, sweet child, and let who will be good." Basil Seal's refugee children, then, in *Put Out More Flags,* are not funny, nor intended to be funny, but the triumph of wickedness (Basil Seal's) over virtue is first-class satire. These hideous children are evil's knout.

Both in Aymé and in Waugh the mask of virtue is ripped away, and other masks. "Thus he would watch in the asparagus season a dribble of melted butter on a woman's chin, marring her beauty and making her look ridiculous, while she would still talk and smile and turn her head, not knowing how she appeared to him." "Her make-up was haphazard and garish, rather like a later Utrillo." Somebody else's war paint is "sploshy, like a John portrait." But it is an impartial process. Even Saint Helena is made tolerable only by being presented as a Miserere Mei in her youth and a bit of a fool in her old age. We remember her reply to the Holy Father when she told him that she was going off to find the True Cross. "You will tell me, will you not," he says with the gentlest irony, "if you are successful?" She cries, "I'll tell the world!" One notes, however, that there is no venom in the unmasking, no bitter hate. One of Waugh's pet aversions is the higher intellectual. He does not rend the creature; he is content to describe his miserable surroundings, his dreary flat, his bath water oozing sadly from that Edwardian collection of verdigris-green viscera called the hot-water geyser which at best gives a niggardly trickle of warm water and at worst explodes in clouds of poisonous vapor. He permits himself only one brief and impartial comment: "But apparatus of this nature is the hallmark of the higher intellectual the world over." He pulls the legs of Catholics when Ambrose Silk, disguised as an Irish priest, is fleeing to Ireland. "Have you a breviary?" his friend asks, examining the disguise for verisimilitude in details. Ambrose says he has not. His friend says, "Oh, well, then, be reading a racing paper!" But the really important unmasking is that of the life of the young people of his decade, whom he presents not so much with paternal bitterness as with brotherly exasperation, always assuaged — or so one may feel — by his honest memory of how much he enjoyed their company while the going was good. For all through his work the subaudible implications suggest certain foiled desires, certain ideals, a certain norm which, he feels, their lives denied, so that one gradually begins to see that his way of presenting them involves what music-hall

comedians call the double take. We laugh, and then the
rubber band slaps back in our faces and we realize that the
laugh is on us. While he is making us laugh over the follies
of these young people, even inducing in us some sympathy
with their rebellion against their elders, their general disillusion, their dissatisfaction with what Miss Elizabeth
Bowen has called the "edited" life of conventional society,
we begin to realize that Waugh is also revealing that he is
disillusioned over their disillusionment and rebelling against
their revolt. He is seeing through them just as clearly as he
insists on seeing through a garish make-up. He sees that their
revolt is negative, their lives are prodigal, they are just as
incapable of any clear concept of a desirable image or way
of life as their fathers, against whom they are in revolt.
That scene in which Miss Runcible dies while all her gay
friends sit around her bed cracking jokes, exchanging gossip
and drinking champagne, unaware that she is sinking into
oblivion, could be taken as a symbol of Waugh's basically
moral criticism of the twenties, whose kiss is death.

It is not that there is anything much that is positively
wrong about them; it is that their lives are fatally negative.
As we watch them we may feel side by side with Hemingway in *The Sun Also Rises*, which comments in the same
spirit on the American expatriates in Paris and Spain between 1918 and the Depression. These amusing, often delightful young people of Waugh's satires were not without
their own earnestness, their own longings, their own idealism, but, to borrow from Camus's *L'Homme Revolté*, they
can only gyrate in the realm of rebellion, incoherently,
emotionally, without ever advancing into the realm of those
ideas which belong to creative revolt. So they waste life,

managing it so loosely. Their damnation is a deprivation, an absence, a vacuity, like Marlowe's hell. In those wild days and nights of the twenties it must have sometimes occurred to Waugh, as it did to Lawrence, that they were all "done for," that at any moment the clock would strike and the chorus come in chanting to the jazz drums of falling bombs and clattering ack-ack:

> *Cut is the branch that might have grown full straight*
> *And burnèd is Apollo's laurel bough.*

In his early and, I think, best books Waugh said none of this — he was much too finely equilibrated a humorist to utter explicit statements, and so long as he could imply his norm he apparently felt no urge to project a positive hero to represent it. This reticence delighted his generation and continues to delight us, as it will probably delight every generation to come. It is the mark of the moral satirist who, like all universal moralists, has detached himself from the accidentals of life by withdrawing to the remote ground of principles so general that — as I have suggested by the comparison with the novels of Marcel Aymé — they could be equally acceptable to people of another nation, and of another time.

This admirable detachment disappeared with the publication of *Brideshead Revisited,* in which Mr. Waugh changed ground. Ceasing to be a moral satirist, he became a writer of romances. We, his devoted readers, had to make, and were not always able to make, a rapid adjustment of our expectations, and if we were his critics, were called on to apply totally different standards. At this distance it is easier to do both things, to recognize that this is not (to understate) another funny book, that it is solemn and serious, romantic and nostalgic, exclusive and personal, and, far from being general in its application, relies to a most disturbing degree on its appeal to our interest through accidental and irrelevant detail. It is this last point which strikes one the most forcibly, as may be seen at once if we retell the story without the accidentals.

One Charles Ryder meets a young man named Flyte, and through him his family. The father and mother have separated. They had both been religious-minded people, the mother being specially pious, but the father abandoned his religion when he left his wife to live with his mistress. The mother dies midway through the book. There are four children. Young Flyte and his sister Julia have reacted from their mother; his brother and his sister remain close to her. Flyte becomes a dipsomaniac, driven to drink, one might say, by the insistent morality of his mother. Julia marries a thrusting Canadian, outside the church of her origin, has an affair with somebody unnamed, falls in love with Ryder, and proceeds to divorce her Canadian husband. When the father ultimately returns home to die, Julia is so affected by seeing him, at the point of his final coma, bless himself that she refuses to marry Ryder, breaks off the proposed marriage, and, we are to understand, returns to the religion of her parents. Ryder, an agnostic, is impressed and begins to take an interest in religion. When the war breaks out, the old home is taken over by the military.

Such a summary, like all summaries, cannot, of course, even remotely suggest the manner in which Waugh has treated his story, or the sort of life he has infused into these bare bones: it can help only to define a subject which a dozen writers might treat in a dozen different ways. Waugh has written his story in a mood of such nostalgic heartache for old things passing or passed away, in a style so tender and fondling, given his chief characters such picturesque backgrounds and so much inherited wealth and traditional grace that one could not quarrel, even while one winced, with Miss Rose Macaulay's choice of the word "lushness" to describe the general effect of surfeit. It would be unjust not to say that he also showed that he possessed hitherto unexpected technical resources for the handling of extended scenes and complex moods: to give only one instance, the swift sketching-in of Ryder's relationship with his wife, and the unstated but clearly felt suggestion of his own state of mind, at the beginning of Book Two is a masterly development of the old quickie technique of disconnected snapshots. Indeed, the chief development in this novel is from disjunction to smoothness — perhaps too much smoothness. Yet, technique apart, how much of his treatment of the essential subject amounts to unessential trappings! It is quite irrelevant, to give a dozen examples, that young Flyte is Lord Sebastian Flyte; that he is a lovely, epicene young man of the nineties with engagingly eccentric ways, such as his devotion to his Teddy bear Aloysius; that he and Ryder meet amid the golden glories of Oxford; that his father is a marquis, his home a beautiful country house, and that he lives now with an Italian mistress in a Venetian palace; that Julia is Lady Julia, or that she marries a man who becomes a cabinet minister; that her love affair with Ryder begins aboard a liner, first class, during a storm, in the environment of roses, masseuse oil and champagne; that Lord Sebastian becomes a dipsomaniac not among the pubs of

Camden Town but in the low dives of Fez. All this is romantic embroidery; a harmless pleasure for the reader, just as it is a pleasure to listen to well-bred people talking in a well-dressed play about something else besides the mist that does be on the bog, or fish-and-chips, or rearmament, moral or otherwise. But when we have passed through these accidentals to what seems at first sight to be the core of the novel, its insistently pervasive Catholicism, it is with a shock of dismay that we gradually realize that this is the most irrelevant accidental of all. In fact, if I may be permitted to give my own personal reaction to the novel as a professing Catholic (adding in all humility that there may be something wrong with my idea of Catholicism), I fail to see why the book could not have been equally well written — admittedly with a very different setting — by a fervent Congregationalist. Had, for instance, the author of *Mark Rutherford's Autobiography* written *Brideshead Revisited* as *Tanner's Lane Revisited* we might have been not only just as impressed, but perhaps more deeply impressed, had he done with it what he did with the *Autobiography*, that is, turned the accidental or immediate subject of his inherited faith into the universal theme of any man's struggles and tensions with any religious dogma whatsoever. This seems to be the essential question. Does Waugh universalize his theme, or does he move within an enclosed and exclusive circle of limited appeal?

What is his theme? If it is that there is no happiness on earth without God, no member of any theistic religion would deny it. If it is that God lures us back to him by ways obscure and strange, a Mohammedan would not deny it. If it is the "twitch on the thread" which can pull men back from the

ends of the earth, from the deepest jungles of indifference
and vice to the ways of virtue, the validity of the observation
is almost devastatingly universal. It applies to so many pulls,
such as patriotism and love. It may, for all one knows, work
powerfully with the Salvation Army. Any novel dealing with
any of these themes, and they all occur in *Brideshead
Revisited,* must, if it proposes to show how they operate
inside one particular religion, throw a piercing light on the
specific quality, power and appeal of that religion, or show
them operating in such a way as to impress equally an
atheist, an agnostic or a member of any church in the world.
Otherwise, obviously, its appeal is not universal. My feeling
is that Waugh has not fully succeeded in doing either of
these things, and for the reason I have stated — that he has
abandoned his detachment, to which I would here add that
he has abandoned it through an excess of loyalty.

For the first, would, say, a Mohammedan reading the
novel understand the power and the appeal of Catholicism?
He would certainly have to acknowledge its power, since it
is so clearly stated — which is not the same thing as to understand it. Its emotional appeal he could not possibly understand. Even I, who happen to be a Catholic, fail to see the
appeal of any such religion as is here depicted, if for no
other reason than that it has brought the minimum of happiness to the maximum number of people; and I do not
speak of happiness in a worldly sense. Nor can it be argued
that the lives of the Marquis, Lord Sebastian or Lady Julia
show that if Catholics are unhappy it is only because they do
not practice their religion. The mother is a devout Catholic:
she appears throughout as a most melancholy woman who is

hated by her husband and who has driven her son to drink. Her elder son, Brideshead, also a devout Catholic, is as somber a figure as one would willingly take a day's march to avoid. To Cordelia, the younger daughter, religion is indeed a tower of strength and consolation and our Mohammedan reader must feel that a faith so powerful to console and bestow inner joy is something to envy. But the most contented person of all is Cara, the mistress of the Marquis, who has learned in the lighthearted Italian way to wear her religion easily and rely on the infinite goodness of God. If Mr. Waugh were writing propaganda for the Catholic Church, she is the woman most likely of all to convert our heathen friend. (Why does everybody who writes about religion concentrate on being miserable about it?)

The theme, as we have seen, is universally valid; the treatment is not. In effect it is reduced from godliness to obedience. Consider the turning point in the whole story, which is centrally the story of Charles Ryder and Julia Flyte. It occurs when Brideshead is telling Ryder and his sister of his intention to marry a Catholic widow; referring to his sister's marriage, outside the church, to the divorced Canadian Rex Mottram, he says roughly that his future wife would not possibly live in the same house as Julia: "It is a matter of indifference whether you choose to live in sin with Rex or Charles or both — I have always avoided inquiry into the details of your menage — but in no case would Beryl consent to be your guest." The result of this bombshell is a harrowing emotional outbreak from Julia in a long speech delivered to Ryder, alone, on the subject of her sin:

"All in one word, too, one little, flat, deadly word that covers a lifetime.

"'Living in sin'; not just doing wrong, as I did when I went to America; doing wrong, knowing it is wrong, stopping doing it, forgetting. That's not what they mean. That's not Bridey's pennyworth. He means just what it says in black and white.

"*Living in sin,* with sin, by sin, for sin, every hour, every day, year in and year out. Waking up with sin in the morning, slipping diamonds to it, feeding it, showing it round, giving it a good time, putting it to sleep at night with a tablet of Dial if it's fretful.

"Always the same, like an idiot child carefully nursed, guarded from the world. 'Poor Julia,' they say, 'she can't go out. She's got to take care of her little sin. A pity it ever lived,' they say, 'but it's so strong. Children like that always are. Julia's so good to her little, mad sin.'"

Then her speech rises to a wild threnody for Christ dying with her sin, over the bed in the night nursery, in the dark little study at Farm Street with the shining oilcloth, in dark churches where the charwoman's brush is raising dust and one candle burns; and so on to the thought of a never-to-be-comforted Christ, a Christ never given shelter, always hanging there, outcast, a citizen of the bare stone and the dust and the smoldering dumps, thrown away there, poked at after nightfall by an old man with lupus carrying a forked stick, "nameless and dead, like the baby they wrapped up and carried away before I had seen her." The scene ends with her lashing her agnostic lover across the face with a switch because he has said something that she thinks stupid and lacking in sympathy and understanding. It is a painful and impressive scene. Yet, what was this frightful sin? To everybody except to Roman Catholics or High Anglicans

divorce is specifically a Roman Catholic sin; a sin of dis-
obedience; a theological sin; a sin against the Council of
Trent; a sin argued about over many centuries; an institutional sin; a club sin. They will feel deeply for Julia, but
they will also feel like outsiders looking in. They must feel
this even more during those long, professional arguments, at
the end, when Marchmain is dying, about the efficacy of
Extreme Unction for a semiconscious, if not virtually unconscious, man.

A religious theme given institutional treatment is always
liable to get lost in the embroidered folds of ecclesiasticism;
and so is the author. The old detachment is sold to loyalty,
and while one admires loyalty there is no place for it in art,
just as there is no place for it in philosophy — or for that
matter in mathematics. The team spirit breeds loyalty, but
artists and philosophers (and mathematicians) do not work
in teams. In reading *Brideshead* one wrings one's hands
when Waugh's loyalty to the aristocratic spirit makes him
say of the family history given to Ryder by Lady Marchmain — a "family history typical of the Catholic squires
of England" — "These men must die to make a world for
Hooper; they were the aborigines, vermin by right of law,
to be shot off at leisure so that things might be safe for
the travelling salesman, with his polygonal pince-nez,
his fat wet hand-shake, his grinning dentures" — Hooper
being the harmless representative in his novel of the cruder
postwar world nowadays satirized by writers like Mr. John
Wain and Mr. Kingsley Amis. The point is not that one
disagrees or agrees with Waugh about the superiority of
the Catholic squires of England to the non-Catholic sales-
men of England; the point is that this is not the snarling

way for any man of letters, least of all for so gifted a satirist, to make any point whatever. One must only feel that in *Brideshead*, whether dealing with church or class, Waugh has allowed himself to be drawn into the whirlpool of his subject. He became his own Undine, killing with a kiss. The moralist, losing his detached standpoint, died, and so did his satire. Where the changeling Waugh went to nobody knows, but he cannot really be far away: he has returned with *The Loved One* and some splendid sequences in his last two novels.

Yet, here again loyalties dominate, and he is again arguing against himself. His natural, instinctive, inherited position was that those same times which destroyed the traditional nobility eliminated the traditional hero. Hungry for both, he has concentrated in *Men at Arms* and *Officers and Gentlemen* on the professional hero (as in *Brideshead* on the professional Catholic), who is, it is quite true, a well-known and highly valued type in the British Army: the well-bred, utterly loyal, utterly fearless Catholic public-school man. Apart from the fact that the area is once again as enclosed and circumscribed as a Henty novel, Waugh's loyalty in response to loyalty is seen to be patiently excessive and destructive of detachment by the fact that all his wealth of satire is reserved for commoners and there is not a glimmer of humor in his picture of Guy Crouchback, who, by a shift of angle, such as Stendhal commanded, must appear as a character with endless comic possibilities. It does not even seem to occur to him that from the point of view and in the language of Crouchback's fellow officers and superiors, he must have often appeared as a pain in the neck. It must be that although there is room and room enough for humor on the subject of loyalty, humor is another one of those pursuits in which there is no room for loyalty. But few humorists have a sense of humor about everything. Most have no sense of humor about themselves.

Waugh is a writer of a pure, instinctive genius which he has amplified by the possession or development of enormous technical skill. He was born with the natural gift for satire. His satires will probably live as long as literature lasts. And he has written seven of them! What an achievement that is one may realize by trying to think offhand of seven other comic novels by seven other individual English writers. Being a man of genius, he should never, under any circumstances, have opinions, for whenever he has written out of his opinions it becomes all too plain all over again that imagination is a soaring gull and opinions no more than a gaggle of ungainly starlings, chattering angrily on a cornfield. Opinions breed anger, nourish hate, ossify the heart, narrow the mind.

> *An intellectual hatred is the worst,*
> *So let her think opinions are accursed.*
> *Have I not seen the loveliest woman born*
> *Out of the mouth of Plenty's horn,*
> *Because of her opinionated mind*
> *Barter that horn and every good*
> *By quiet natures understood*
> *For an old bellows full of angry wind?*

He has what Yeats wished for his daughter, a "radical innocence . . . self-delighting, self-appeasing, self-affrighting." He did not receive it from ancestry, or from this class or that, from church or university; he did not build it out of ideas, or theories. It is one of Nature's primal gifts. But it can be lost, and it can commit suicide. It can poison itself. Thinking is pure poison to innocence. Huxley, who never knew innocence, thrives on thought. But Waugh? One recalls what Cocteau said of Mistinguett, that she magnificently reversed Descartes's *Cogito, ergo sum* into *Mais je ne pense jamais! Donc je suis!*

GRAHAM GREENE

I suffer, therefore I am

THE two most striking things about the novels of Graham Greene are their preoccupation with evil and their intellectual *jusqu'au-boutisme*. As for the latter, one is reminded of Camus's declaration that it is not sufficient to live, we must have and perceive a destiny that does not wait on death: man, that is, wants to anticipate his own destiny, and every writer wants to express in terms of this world the mortal destiny of man. It is a modern attitude among novelists. They were formerly satisfied to bring their novels to an intermediate destination rather than to expound an ultimate destiny. Marriage, love, domestic happiness, self-completion, self-fulfillment, self-perfection are in one way or another the themes of Balzac, Scott, Dickens, Stendhal and Tolstoy; whereas it has been well said that Greene, Mauriac and Bernanos return us to the medieval world, as if the great humanist tradition had never happened. Where Dante saw the totality of human destiny as a vision outside the flaming ramparts of the world, men like Greene bring the other world into this present life. If this has, as I intend to suggest, the effect of disintegrating his characters, of liquefying them, possibly of dehumanizing them, it also has the fine effect of enlarging the imaginative and visionary content of his work. It explains, at any rate, his extremism, his reckless courage in taking an idea to the limits of its implications. (He does this nowhere more fully than in *The Heart of the Matter.*) It is something which fills the sensitive reader with apprehension. "Whither next?" one asks, and wonders when he will come up against a stone wall, or a chasm.

His obsession with the ugly and evil side of life is equally troubling. More than occasionally one feels that he is not merely outraging nature but that he is taking a perverse pleasure in rubbing its face in its own ordure. One feels that in concentrating on a restricted set of themes he has implied that no matter what subject he may choose to paint — childhood innocence, mother love, a first kiss — he could make it look just as grim. Not, of course, that anybody has the least right to object to grimness, and every writer is entitled to wear whatever spectacles he pleases. But one may, indeed must, if necessary, draw attention to the limitations of an artist's palette, or of his human sympathy, or of his intellectual interests. One may, if necessary, draw a distinction between an intellectual approach and a pathological obsession. I feel that more than a few of Greene's books justify our apprehension on all these counts; that his attitude to life exists, like the mental world of Pascal, so close to the border

line of the morbid and corrupt as to be saved from both only
by the utmost delicacy and restraint; and much of Greene's
work, to my mind, shows small signs that he is sufficiently
aware of the importance of these sanitary precautions.

It must be clear to us all by now — he has made it clear —
that his attraction to evil and ugliness was originally instinctive or emotional, and that he has gradually built about
it an intellectual scaffolding. It is the natural way of the
artist: first feeling, then perception. Evil and ugliness inspire
him. They are the compost of his flower garden. Faith, for
him, is not a gift; it is won from despair. Love relies on the
validity of hate. His hope of heaven depends on the reality
of hell. He believes in God because he believes in Satan.
That it is an uncomfortable and not very attractive approach does not invalidate it; and it is not entirely alien to
the English tradition — one thinks at once of Bunyan. Indeed, there is nothing absolutely startling or new about it.
Man has always cried to the Lord *de profundis*, and moralists
have frequently observed that the most direct road to godliness may be the road that seems to lead the other way.
Pierre Emmanuel said it simply in his *Autobiography* when
he declared that it is not morality but immorality (ugliness
and evil) that brings us to God — the nauseating experience
of finding ourselves face to face with our own naked shame
and stale self-disgust. Yet few writers have found so much
positive satisfaction, even comfort, in the sight of evil as
Greene has. Joyfully he reverses Browning. God's in his
heaven, all's wrong with the world. He *has* to be in his
heaven. Conversely, whenever Greene sees people happy in
their vulgar, cheery, beery way he is filled with gloom. No
good, he seems to say, can possibly come of happiness.

He has been explicit about this in the opening pages of
The Lawless Roads, that entirely dreary book about Mexico
which, in passing, is as good an illustration as any of his less
successful books of the danger of sticking too rigidly to a
narrow point of view. The first two pages of the book will
suffice:

I was, I suppose, thirteen years old. Otherwise why should
I have been there — in secret — on the dark croquet lawn? I
could hear the rabbit moving behind me, munching the grass
in his hutch; an immense building with small windows,
rather like Keble College, bounded the lawn. It was the
school; from somewhere behind it, from across the quad,
came a faint sound of music: Saturday night, the school or-
chestra was playing Mendelssohn. I was alone in mournful happiness in the dark. Two countries just here lay side
by side. From the croquet lawn, from the raspberry canes,
from the greenhouse and the tennis lawn you could always
see — dominatingly — the great square Victorian buildings of
garish brick: they looked down like skyscrapers on a small
green countryside where the fruit trees grew and the rab-
bits munched. You had to step carefully: the border was
close beside your gravel path. From my mother's bedroom
window — where she had borne the youngest of us to the
sound of school-chatter and the disciplinary bell — you
looked straight down into the quad, where the hall and the
chapel and the classrooms stood. If you pushed open a green
baize door in a passage by my father's study, you entered
another passage deceptively similar, but none the less you
were on alien ground. There would be a slight smell of io-
dine from the matron's room, of damp towels from the
changing rooms, of ink everywhere. Shut the door behind
you again, and the world smelt differently: books and
fruit and eau-de-Cologne.

One was an inhabitant of both countries: on Saturday and

Sunday afternoons on one side of the baize door, the rest of
the week on the other. How can life on a border be other
than restless? You are pulled by different ties, of hate and
love. For hate is quite as powerful a tie: it demands allegiance. In the land of the skyscrapers, of stone stairs and
cracked bells ringing early, one was aware of fear and hate,
a kind of lawlessness — appalling cruelties could be practised
without a second thought; one met for the first time characters, adult and adolescent, who bore about them the genuine quality of evil. There was Collifax, who practised tor-
ments with dividers; Mr. Cranden with three grim chins, a
dusty gown, a kind of demoniac sensuality; from these
heights evil declined towards Parlow, whose desk was
filled with minute photographs — advertisements of art
photos. Hell lay about them in their infancy.

One pauses at this parody of Wordsworth. Does "hate"
demand "allegiance"? Surely there is a confusion of mind
here. The *person* or *thing* one loves or hates may demand
allegiance: school, drink, the object for which one longs or
lusts. When a man says he must have love, he means either
that he must have somebody to love truly, or somebody with
whom to fornicate; and to the one he must give "allegiance,"
but must he to the other? It is a curious, and, I think, re-
vealingly obsessional, choice of word. The memory proceeds:

There lay the horror and the fascination. One escaped surreptitiously for an hour at a time: unknown to frontier
guards, one stood on the wrong side of the border looking
back — one should have been listening to Mendelssohn, but
instead one heard the rabbit restlessly cropping near the
croquet hoops. It was an hour of release — and also an
hour of prayer. One became aware of God with an intensity
— time hung suspended — music lay on the air; anything
might happen before it became necessary to join the crowd

across the border. There was no inevitability anywhere . . .
faith was almost great enough to move mountains . . . the
great buildings rocked in the darkness.

And so faith came to one — shapelessly, without dogma, a
presence above a croquet lawn, something associated with
violence, cruelty, evil across the way. One began to believe
in heaven because one believed in hell.

It is fascinating, and it is frightening. Thereafter will the
boy ever be able to do without "hell"? Will it become: "One
believes in heaven only because one believes in hell"? Will
everything that is not heaven have to become hell? It begins
to seem so. For from there the memory goes on to give us a
strange picture of a little country town in Hertfordshire set
in pastoral country within a crescent of the Chiltern hills.
I must have passed through or paused at this rather pleasant-
looking town a dozen times before. One afternoon, halting at
one of the pubs for a drink, and observing a couple of men
who were obviously schoolmasters chatting amiably over a
beer, I realized that this was the hideous town anathematized
in the opening pages of *The Lawless Roads*. Everything in
Greene's description of it is in the manner of Joyce's impressions of a Dublin slum. Our attention is directed to a
shabby shop selling *London Life,* with the usual "articles
about high heels, corsets and long hair" (for men, one
presumes); to the fake Tudor Café where four one-armed
men dine together, "arranging their seats so that their arms
shouldn't clash" — which, one may observe, most two-armed
people also do; we are told about "Irish servant girls
making assignations for a ditch" — and one wonders how
Greene could know. The most seemingly innocent things are
made to seem cheap or sinister. When a girl is observed

cutting some branches off a tree, she does so "with an expression abased and secretive." The saw "wails" through the wood. The photographs in a shop window become "yellowing faces," and they "peer out" at passers-by. When somebody pushes in the door of the Plough Inn, it chimes; ". . . ivory balls clicked, and a bystander said, 'they do this at the Crown, Margate' — England's heart beating out in bagatelle to her eastern extremity." He quotes newspaper reports about a murder; about the suicide of a girl of fifteen, pregnant with a second child that might have been the child of any one of fourteen youths; which is the first really shocking thing, apart from *London Life,* that has been mentioned. Even the game of Monopoly, very popular hereabouts, we are told — as if it were not popular at the time in a dozen languages — is presented as a sign of a grasping, selfish world without any sense of responsibility for seduced children, early divorces or the ancient soil abused by new bungalows. "You couldn't live," we are told, "in a place like this; it was somewhere to which you returned for sleep and rissoles by the 6.50 or the 7.25."

Obviously, common sense tells us, all this exists, or for hell's sake is made to exist, only in his own lacerated imagination. One sympathizes sincerely. The place is evidently associated with some deep, unhealed traumatic wound. But one suspects that when he sets off for the wilds of Mexico (to which this is the prologue) he will find everything just as squalid and heartless. He does. All he has to do is to change the names and the circumstances: the impression is in the same color, a general rot-green light. The only important difference is that he implies, not very persuasively, that if the Mexican people were allowed to practice their old religion in complete freedom, life there would be less squalid. To which one can only reply that nobody is hunting down Catholics with police dogs in Hertfordshire. But it would be pointless to argue rationally about all this, since the man is clearly not talking about objective conditions at all. We must agree, however, that it is an achievement to be able to see the devil in unlikely places, for he doubtless is everywhere. Mauriac has not a finer nose for Satan. Pascal had not a finer ear when he heard the voice of Beelzebub among the Jesuits than Greene hearing the authentic whisper of eternal corruption in the chiming doorbell of the Plough Inn and the innocent flick of billiard balls. This is real tin-chapel stuff. Bunyan suffered the same agonies in the Bedford pubs.

We can understand so much without difficulty; but two puzzles suggest themselves. It is good to see evil on many sides if it helps to remind us constantly that good and godliness are just around the corner. Why, however, must they always be around the corner, never walking down the High Street? It is also good to be able to show, if one persuasively can, that there is no real essential difference between native and foreign forms of evil: that nobody living in the home counties has the right to be smugly horrified by the affairs of Chiapas or Tabasco, with priests hiding in swamps and being shot when found there, hotel lavatories ankle-deep in ordure, flies that produce a hideous form of blindness, dead beetles lying on the floor being devoured by long processions of hungry ants, buzzards on tin roofs, and so forth and so on. But, if wherever one goes — London, Brighton, Mexico, Stockholm, Vienna, Stamboul, Indochina — one will always find the same story, why stir at all? The answer evokes what may be the essential question: that although it is true that whenever a moralist writes he describes a *voyage autour de son âme,* why does no other moralist bring back such a consistently identical story? Greene must then be some special sort of moralist; whereupon the essential questions arise: What is his sort? What is his tradition?

I suggest that the only comparable modern analogy is with Pascal and Jansenism. It is a literary tradition which has exercised a much more far-reaching influence on the course of modern literature than we commonly realize. Essentially its challenge has been felt as a challenge to the humanists to deny, and prove, that there is not an impassable gulf between pleasure and the virtuous life, between the weakness of human nature and its possibilities of greatness, between all that we like to enjoy and most of the things we pretend to admire. In its heyday it provoked a profound opposition, and when Port-Royal fell, it might all seem to have been no more than a flash in the pan. But Pascal did not come out of nothing, and when one is discussing the French nature, it is still one of the more agreeable problems to ask what in the French nature produced him. Perhaps it is enough to say that the pessimism of Jansenism is endemic in human nature in general. We may think back to Saint Augustine and the Manichaeans, to go no further. What is more to our purpose is to observe how persistently it recurs; the power of an appealing literary form — every French writer must have read and admired Pascal — to keep ideas alive; and the historical fact that the rise of Jansenism coincided with the beginnings of the whole modern high-minded disapproval of aristocratic irresponsibility.

I do not suggest that many writers swallow Pascal whole. But he does seem to offer something to a great many types of writers — the ascetically minded Catholic, the natural skeptic with no interest in religion (La Rochefoucauld was of the type), the soured hedonist, the frustrated romantic, the earnest social reformer, the topical satirist. The list of candidates for the title of neo-Pascalians in our time is long: Bernanos, Julian Green, Mauriac, Céline, Marcel Aymé, Camus, Faulkner, Moravia, George Orwell, Graham Greene — all of them antihumanist, antiheroic, highly skeptical about man's inherent dignity, which the great humanist tradition took as the cornerstone of all its beliefs, full of misgivings as to the nature of free will.

We had here better redefine our terms, since Jansenism is one of those words that has been so loosely used — almost as a term of common abuse without any precise meaning, like Pink, or Liberal, or Left, or Romantic — that anybody using it as a term of literary criticism is under an obligation to say what precisely he means by it. The word, we will recall, originated quite simply out of an exchange of ideas between the Abbé Saint-Cyran and Jansen, Bishop of Ypres, with a view to a reform within the Catholic Church. The main documents are *Augustinus,* which is a sort of anthology of relevant Augustiniana — Saint Augustine being taken as a representative of the more extreme, though orthodox, view on the doctrine of Grace, which was the cardinal point involved — various records of the imprint the doctrine left on the convent of Port-Royal; the writings of Pascal, especially the *Lettres provinciales,* that highly entertaining book in which one may watch the fight between the Jansenists and the Jesuits as close up as in television; and the continuing marks of its influence well on into the eighteenth century in La Rochefoucauld, Racine, Boileau and others.

From these we gather that the central Jansenist doctrine was that man cannot be saved by his own efforts. Alone he is helpless. He depends for salvation on the arbitrary, if not actually capricious, gift of Grace, which he can neither achieve of his own efforts nor, if it is granted to him, resist.

I am simplifying a good deal here. One might mention for a larger view the distinctions made between various kinds of Grace, such as what Catholic theologians call "sufficent Grace"; or the Grace which suffices to enable a man to choose well, and which will fail only when he deliberately refuses to co-operate. Jansen denied its existence. To him, if a man failed, it was only because he had not been given enough assistance from his Creator, which of course means the end of free will. One might put this simply by saying that, to Jansen, if a man had been granted Grace amounting to only fifty-nine volts and if he had to face a temptation equal to sixty volts, all was up with him; if it was the other way round, then Beelzebub was helpless. Both deny free will. Indeed, logically, the commandments become impossible of fulfillment within this savage doctrine. One can see how utterly it deflates human dignity, confidence and self-pride.

The social and historical origins of Jansenism are also relevant. Its rise coincided with the growing absolutism of Louis XIV, the corresponding decline of aristocratic power, so resolutely assailed by Mazarin and Richelieu, and the corresponding rise of a bourgeoisie antipathetic to the aristocrats' lavish attitude to life in general. One can understand how Jansenism with its stress on self-discipline, prudence and forethought would appeal to the bourgeois conscience. The strange thing is that it did not appeal more to the

bourgeois sense of moderation. The princes of the Church
certainly did not consider it a moderate doctrine: they had
learned on too many battlefields that while it is all very well
to remind us that as compared with our Creator we are
brute beasts, there is always the danger that we may take
it so much to heart as to act on it. The Church knew that
nothing corrupts like excess. Pascal knows no such benevolence. He rubs man's face into the mud. *"La grandeur de
l'homme est grande en ce qu'il se connait misérable."* Even
after he has received the gift of divine Grace he does not
alter his nature — though he may change his object.

The probable effects of such a doctrine on literature seem
evident. What price glory now? It becomes mere self-love.
One might even argue that Pascal is a sort of theological
forerunner of egalitarianism; as when in his *Trois Discours
sur la Condition des Grands* he rails against the people who
think that the great ones of the earth are in any real sense
great.* Man as Hero could not, evidently, long survive such
an attitude. If we are subject to all those weaknesses with
which Pascal makes such play, our inconstancy, our self-
contradictions, our temperament, our credulity, all our palpitating sensibilities, we are not masters of our fates but
slaves of chance, blind instruments of our own vanities.
Inevitably, in this dispensation, the Corneillian concept of
man as Hero — to the Jansenists at once absurd and sinful
— gave way to Racine and the theme of fated passion. It
was to be a hundred years before romantic poetry would
restore the Hero under another form, but, concurrently, the
psychological novel — through Madame de Lafayette, Ben-

---

* In all this I am much indebted to *Morales du Grand Siècle,* by Paul
Bénichou. Paris, 1948.

jamin Constant, de Laclos, Stendhal and so on into the nineteenth century — demonstrates and accelerates what Mr. Martin Turnell has so well called the "disintegration of personality," begun by the Pascalian way of looking at life. One does not, to be sure, deny that this modern disintegration had other origins.

With so much by way of definition let us now turn back to Greene's novels and observe four of their cardinal characteristics.

(1) *The obsessive theme.* It has been said frequently that his obsessive theme is the Hunted Man. This is true only if we take the phrase in the sense of a man hunted by himself: the sense of the epigraph to his first novel *The Man Within:* "There's another man within me that's angry with me." In the literal sense, the hunted man is not the subject of *The End of the Affair, The Heart of the Matter, Brighton Rock* (not the subject, though it is a thread in the story), *It's a Battlefield, Stamboul Train* (unless one strains a point to make Czinner the central character), or *Rumour at Nightfall.* He is the subject of *A Gun for Sale* and *The Power and the Glory.* In any case he is never the theme of Greene's novels.

His persistent theme is betrayal under one form or another: treason, unfaithfulness, the double cross, the letdown, the broken trust. This may be why there is such a strong suggestion of a sense of grievance in all his work, a certain sulkiness in his attitude to life which reminds one of Claude Edmonde Magny's remark about Hemingway, that behind the mask of the hero there is the face of a *pauvre petit garçon,* a little boy whose bun was stolen by somebody when he was very young. Somebody has said that there is no use in playing a game where everybody cheats. Everybody cheats Greene in Greene's world.

Let us test this suggestion that betrayal is his central theme. In *The Man Within* a smuggler betrays his best friend and his fellow smugglers. In *Rumour at Nightfall* two journalists, Crane and Chase, are attracted to the same woman. Crane betrays Chase to her. Chase then betrays Crane to the authorities. The woman thereupon, having married Crane only a few hours before, takes Chase to her heart. The bitter moral of *Stamboul Train* is that faithfulness never pays. Czinner the idealist revolutionary is shot. The honest little trollop Coral Musker is overnight swapped by the businessman Myatt for the quondam Lesbian Janet Purdoe, who thereby betrays her former friend Mabel Warren, who now takes on Coral Musker, after being instrumental in bringing about Czinner's death. In *It's a Battlefield*, where everybody lets down everybody else and gets nothing much out of it, the only conclusion open to us is that unfaithfulness does not pay either. Here Jim Drover, a Communist, is under sentence of death. His wife betrays him, his brother betrays him; Condor, a journalist, betrays his pals; his sister-in-law is unfaithful all round; Surrogate the writer is unfaithful to his dead wife; and the Assistant Commissioner of Police decides in his devotion to the law that he must not be overloyal to justice. In *Brighton Rock* the whole central story of Rose and Pinkie turns on betrayal or the fear of betrayal. Pinkie murders Hale for having betrayed the gang, then betrays Spicer, then seduces Rose lest she should betray him. *The Ministry of Fear,* a war story, is specifically concerned with traitors. In *England Made Me* we are in the world of international finance,

where Kate Farrant is the only really reliable character:
the central figure, Tony Farrant, might truthfully be described as the sort of charm-dispensing liar who would dou-
ble-cross his sister, since that is precisely what he does. In
A Gun for Sale the hare-lipped assassin is double-crossed by
his employers, and any pity we may feel for this murderous
maniac comes from his vain hope that Anne, the detective's
girl, will not give him away to the police, which she has to
do. In *The Heart of the Matter* Scobie is unfaithful to his
wife, lets his mistress down, and his servant, and one may
fairly hold the view that his final gamble for salvation is on
the border line of a double cross on God. But we are given
to understand that God is treated poorly by most of the
characters in these stories. Raven, seeing the infant Christ
in the crib, thinks: There He lies waiting "for the double-
cross, the whip, the nails." This general unfaithfulness is
symbolical of mankind's eternally renewed Judas kiss.

(2) *The denial of free will.* All these characters, we are
made to feel, are coping with circumstances beyond their
power, the dice loaded against them. They are fissurated by
self-interest, self-distrust, self-pity, ambition, lust, greed, fear,
hate, weak longing for peace at any price, and, most dissolvent weakness of all, human respect. They are, indeed,
permitted to have glimpses of the Good Life, but the battle
that takes place within their consciences — where the act
of treason takes place — is a foregone conclusion. It is true
that when we first come to these grim novels we have hopes
that somebody will rise superior to the brute. Once we have
become familiar with the obsessive theme we know that
these brief spurts of gallantry will soon die. For example,
one might, if one did not know the line of fate as Greene

sees it, have, for a while, high hopes that Myatt, in *Stamboul Train,* will delight us by sticking pluckily to the chorus girl Coral. And Greene tries hard to be fair to Myatt, or seems to be trying, though since Myatt, like everybody else in the novel, except Czinner, collapses in the end, one cannot avoid feeling that Greene has given only that he may in the end take away. Or we might hope that Conrad Drover in *It's a Battlefield* will at least succeed in shooting the police commissioner. Knowing the foreordained line of fate, we are sardonically gratified when he merely succeeds in shooting at the commissioner with blank cartridges. Nobody in Greene's novels stands a dog's chance.

Greene was not always so hopeless of humanity. He had a romantic period at the start of his career represented by three novels of which he has since suppressed two. In this period his men were, to be sure, just as prone to evil, but he did allow to some of them gestures of real self-perception, self-truth and final regeneration. I think he may still have hoped at this period that man could save himself. There is a curious passage in *Rumour at Nightfall* which suggests that if he could then see this hope for man it was because he was still seeing life as a conflict of a purely human order. Crane has found out that his beloved Eulalia had previously been the lover of a Spaniard. The discovery pains him, but he nourishes this pain in the belief that without pain truth is of an inferior quality. In pain one discovers oneself. Descartes's "I think, therefore I am" becomes "I suffer, therefore I am." Crane expresses this by calling painless truth "comfortable," whereas those who suffer when they see the truth will not be comfortable, will desire virtue and admiration and courage, even though they may actually in their weakness choose "lies, evasions, compromises, fears and humanity." So Crane by honestly recognizing his own cowardice and suffering achieves a final act of courage.

It would be interesting to know what happened in Graham Greene's mind around 1931; for in that year the romantic-humanist period closed with a bang, as if something that had been gnawing at the foundations of his belief in man's power of self-purification brought down the wall separating him from an almost total despair of human nature. In that year he wrote *Stamboul Train,* and after that the road is clear. The romantic style vanishes. Decorous expression, reticence, the note of human idealism give way, with those nineteenth-century smugglers and Carlists, to the modern scene painted with all that ruthless brutality, brassiness, brilliance, cruelty, sexiness, tartness, satire and so on which he would finally justify so magnificently in *The Power and the Glory* — though, as we shall note, with the new addition of a mystical escape into final optimism.

It is interesting, possibly revealing, that only two types are permitted to engage our sympathy from *Stamboul Train* onward: priests and trollops. Each of these is outside the battle: the priest because he is sold to heaven, the trollop because she is at least undeceived, knows that she is what she is — Greene loathes all forms of pretense, fake, sentimentality, as the surest paths to the Judas kiss — and, knowing herself, may one day re-enter the battle. See also *The End of the Affair.*

Why does Greene load the dice so completely against his characters? It is the old Jansenist reason that man, of himself, can do nothing. Only God can do it. He was already groping towards this idea in his early romantic period. There, in *Rumour at Nightfall,* we come on the frightening observation that "if Judas betrayed God, God betrayed Judas by waiting for his coming." Sin appears to be coercive. People are so caught in the net that even when they would do good they do harm — it is the theme of *The Quiet American* — and if they are godless, must do harm: as when Ida in *Brighton Rock* by her pity for Hale starts a chain of circumstances that brings disaster all round, or when Rose by her human pity for Pinkie drives him still deeper into evil. In *Brighton Rock* he allows us at least the chance of godly help, but it is only a chance, and it remains only a chance thereafter — if it is permissible to think of a last-minute miracle as a chance. Pinkie's only hope is expressed in the far from hopeful verse: "Between the stirrup and the ground he mercy sought — and mercy found." Scobie's gamble in *The Heart of the Matter* seems like a million-to-one chance. He cannot stop desiring Helen; his wife insists on his receiving Communion; his priest can give him no loophole; rather than go on offending God he kills himself. His only hope is that God will forgive self-murder because it was done through love of God.

I confess that when I first read, and reviewed, this novel I complained that the situation was rigged. Greene had manipulated his character into a neurotic state of mind, with a neurotic wife, in a corner of Africa, in a corner of his conscience, with a far from intelligent priest, so that there should be no escape from his problem but suicide. I should add here, for the benefit of non-Catholics, that an intelligent priest should have pointed out his true duty to Scobie: that is, to promise to amend his life and thereafter to go on struggling against the attractions of the flesh. For Scobie to reply that he *knew* that he could not defeat his desires would have been beside the point. Every man in Scobie's position must try endlessly, hoping for the power he momentarily lacks. He could be quite sincere in his efforts, and no priest, however grieved, could refuse him absolution as long as he was honestly trying. Scobie's refusal to go on trying was, in Catholic theology a denial of God's willingness to co-operate on the battlefield, totally at contrast with his final hope that God would co-operate in mercifulness beyond the battlefield. Anyway — though this would seem cynical to Greene's and Scobie's unbending and prideful conscience — if Scobie had to commit any lethal act, why, I asked myself, did Scobie not poison his wife instead of poisoning himself? He could then have married Helen and spent the rest of his life in penance. It would certainly be a frightful deed, and a frightful gamble with salvation, but is murder worse than self-murder? He cherished his wife too dearly? He did not cherish her so dearly as to be faithful to her. And a man is bound to cherish himself just as much as his wife. I now see, however, that Greene was logical and I was not. He did not rig the story as a matter of technique; he rigged it as a matter of principle. Everything he writes is rigged to demonstrate that human nature is rigged against itself. Besides, and this above all, Greene is not in the least interested in finding interim or human solutions to any problem that he poses. He wants situations in which (symbolically) there can be no solutions of a purely human nature.

His play *The Living Room* is a very good example of this rigging on principle. Here a Catholic girl becomes the mistress of an atheist. She is made to live in a house — a world

— where every room but one is symbolically sealed off. In this room she lives, through the play, with two unsympathetic guardians, both very old women, one of them half dotty, and a paralyzed priest chained to a Bath chair whose arguments with the atheist would be unworthy of the rawest seminarian: this in a city not ill supplied with priests of a high intellectual caliber and capable of giving an influential sympathy to any girl in such a situation. All the harassed girl can do, we are asked to accept, is to commit suicide (like Scobie) and at the last second say a prayer remembered from her nursery days. I recall that I left the theater on the first night in a state of rage which, I later recognized, must have been somewhat like the state of irritation into which the seventeenth-century Jansenists threw their Jesuit opponents — men with a sweeter conception of God's world. And, after all, though Jansen did not allow that man has the power, of himself, to choose between good and evil (*libertas contradictionis*), he did at least allow that man is free from external coercion (*libertas coactione*). Greene seems to me to deny this. The weakness of his method of rigging on principle is that it coerces man into sin.

(3) *His belittlement of human nature.* It inevitably follows that Greene tends to reduce man's stature and all his works. It must be unnecessary to give illustrations. I must again insist, however, that we have no right to complain about this. A writer, given a certain *manière de voir*, can only do with it what he can. But we are entitled, and obliged, to consider the resultant technical and moral coercions.

One of these is that Greene by deliberately reducing man's stature, and impugning his free will, for the purposes of his theme, must always be in grave danger of making his people so subservient to his theme that they become its puppets. It must be left to each reader of *Brighton Rock,* for example, to say whether Pinkie strikes them as a human being or as a puppet. I find him entirely unpersuasive except as something strayed out of a mental home. I suggest that the same is true of Raven in *A Gun for Sale.* Everybody in *It's a Battlefield,* with the exception of the boy Jules, is coerced to play a foreordained role. So are the main characters in *England Made Me:* they are credible only as examples of that form of semipathological egotism so neatly intimated by the epigraph from Walt Disney, "All the world owes *me* a living." They are all, like Scobie, vehicles of a preconceived idea. In so far as they come alive they come alive *after* they have been conceived as symbols.

We are forced again and again to the conclusion that Greene is not primarily interested in human beings, human problems, life in general as it is generally lived; that what he is writing is not so much novels as modern miracle plays. It is one of his great achievements that so many people can nevertheless read his novels on the naturalistic level, and be persuaded by them on that level; for he has enormous invention, a graphic eye, one of the quickest minds working in fiction today, and an inflammable and infectious imagination. I can only say that I do not believe that he is interested in the matter of his novels one tenth as much as in their message. In fact, I go so far as to doubt if he is in the least interested in human nature except in so far as he can put it into some weird-looking cabinet, saw it up in bits, stick swords into it, fire shots at it, draw the curtain and show us that it has suddenly been transmogrified magically, or miraculously, if one prefers, into an angel.

One constant coercion that follows from his treatment of mankind is that their power of intelligent thought is gravely impaired: that faculty which lifts us above the limitations of our natures and our circumstances. Nearly all his people are forced therefore to act violently, and to come to disaster. His people feel rather than think. In this he reminds me of Faulkner, whose people are so dominated by an overpowering weight of fate from the past that they can only struggle wildly, violently and disastrously. It was not so much Greene who began to write thrillers in 1931 as his characters, who ran away with him.

(4) *The mystical escape from nature.* There is a second watershed in Greene's career, after 1931. It occurred somewhere around 1938 when, in *Brighton Rock*, he had taken the ordinary thriller technique to the limit. Around that year he became involved by an act of God or chance in a libel action concerning Miss Shirley Temple, then a child actress. While acting as film critic for a humorous paper called *Night and Day*, most unfortunately for himself but fortunately for literature, he chose to intimate that Miss Temple was not so much the darling of her coevals as the *femme fatale* of elderly gentlemen gone a little beyond their sexual prime. Mr. Greene retired to Mexico, wrote *The Lawless Roads,* and found the theme of *The Power and the Glory.*

It is interesting that the first of these books, a factual record, was extremely dull, and the second, a play of imagination on fact, was to prove one of the finest novels of our time in any language. He saw there that far from being a

pessimist in his sensitiveness to the omnipresence of evil
he had all along been a supreme optimist. He had tortured
himself unnecessarily with the squalor of the world's underground annexes — the furtive love-making in suburban back
lanes or under mud-spattered iron bridges in the shadow of
sweet evil-smelling gasometers, the savageries of race-course
gangs, the painted madam, the exhausted whore, the cigarette butt disintegrating in the lavatory bowl, the dead
gangster in his coffin at a peep show, the smutty postcard
passed around under school desks — all the tawdry vicious-
ness of which not merely the scum of humanity but each
one of us, but for the grace of God, is capable. He saw that
what he must do with all this was to magnify it more and
more until it exploded, and there at the center of the foul
explosion would shine the unsullied face of God. Everything for the best in the worst possible world. So, the priest
in *The Power and the Glory*, when dogged by the Judas of
the book and forced to listen to his sordid confession, thinks:

> Man was so limited; he hadn't even the ingenuity to in-
> vent a new vice: the animals knew as much. It was for this
> world that Christ died: the more evil you saw and heard
> about you, the greater glory lay around the death; it was
> too easy to die for what was good and beautiful, for home
> or children or civilisation — it needed a God to die for the
> half-hearted and corrupt.

Indeed, the corruption of mankind is a sort of backhanded
tribute to God; it is even a form of godliness to be corrupt;
or at least to be corrupt does not deprive us of a form of
godliness, as the priest argues in a striking and daring
passage in which he looks down at the dirty, yellow-fanged,
half-caste traitor jogging on a mule at his side and realizes

the implications of the Christian belief that man is made after God's image and likeness:

> But at the centre of his own faith there always stood the convincing mystery — that we are made in God's image — God was the parent, but He was also the policeman, the criminal, the priest, the maniac and the judge. Something resembling God dangled from the gibbet or went into odd attitudes before the bullets in a prison yard or contorted itself like a camel in the attitude of sex. He would sit in the confessional and hear the complicated dirty ingenuities which God's image had thought out: and God's image shook now, up and down on the mule's back, with the yellow teeth sticking out over the lower lip. . . . He pressed his hand with a kind of driven tenderness on the shoulders of God's image.

It is superbly irrational. It is even illogical. Because a maniac is made in God's image, that does not make God a maniac. Since God has no body, it would be anthropomorphic to suggest that his image is bodily. The essence of man's likeness to God is intellectual and spiritual, so that a maniac or a fornicator ceases to act in God's "image" by his behavior. But such a daring and finely imaginative passage is not to be shredded to pieces. It is a sort of poem. It is not to be thought about. It is to be felt with. To be rational about such things is to be either vulgar or satirical. Mr. Evelyn Waugh could invent a delightful character who had read too much Graham Greene and ended up as some sort of specially obscene heretic.

All Graham Greene's best work can only be read as "a sort of poem," an exciting blend of realism as to its detail and poetry as to its conception. It is not only the brainless and predestined quality of his characters that makes them move so fast: they have been conceived under the emotional pressure of poetic inspiration which flies them as high as maddened kites. In this sense, Greene's characters really are hunted men, the hounds of heaven at their heels. It is one significant reason why they are least interesting when they pause. Then they come down to earth, to common life, and common life is a range of experience beyond Greene's powers, since it is outside his interest.

In *The Power and the Glory*, it will be remembered, the priest halts in his flight when, in a moment of weakness, he decides to dodge his fate. It is the one section of the novel in which he fails to hold us. The mystical escape from common human nature has been, so to speak, switched off. When the priest resumes his journey to his Gethsemane, the voltage of the novel at once comes up again. So, one of the finest scenes in the novel occurs when he is, while trying to buy wine for the Mass, arrested as a bootlegger and thrown into jail. That night scene in the jail, stinking with moral and bodily ordure, when, in the foul darkness among criminals, he at last publicly admits that he is a priest, and they, the lowest of the low, do not betray him, is one of the finest scenes in all fiction.

In Greene as in much of modern fiction the hero has given place to the martyr. Greene lives vicariously the broken lives of the betrayed ones of the earth. We, with whatever degree of misgiving as to his ideas about betrayal, partake in this general martyrdom, very much as we do also when we read Faulkner, or Hemingway, or Aymé, or Joyce, whose heroes are broken, or "betrayed," by a more human sort of enemy than Greene's Jansenistic invention of innate evil. In a strange and deeply moving sense Greene suffers crucifixion for his characters' sakes. Not that he can hope to redeem them. Within his philosophy the redemption of man by Christ is perpetually thwarted by innate evil. All he can give to us is a final hope, not intense, far from heartening, that our immortal destiny may be greater than our mortal deserts; but that we have small hope of release or even relief from the bondage of sin and the devil here below, the whole burthen of his work gloomily asserts. Sweetness and light are hereafter, or not at all. Pascal would have sympathized with this sad message, however shocked by the author's method of presentation.

I have not attempted to conceal that, over the years, I have grown a little weary both of Greene's message and his methods. If one compares his work with Mauriac's, one will see that he has sacrificed too much to both. All Mauriac's best work keeps a fine balance between his humanity and his beliefs. He knows that if his beliefs do not demonstrate themselves in the ordinary world of ordinary people they cannot demonstrate themselves persuasively at all. So, the mental and emotional processes of the husband in *A Knot of Vipers* are purely human processes. They are recognizable and persuasive in proportion as they are human and normal processes. His characters are ridden by fierce passions, but they deal with their own passions, succumb to them or surmount them, as apparently fully rounded human beings. (In his weaker later novels, the puppet master's fingers are sadly visible.) His work has a corresponding variety. I do not find this variety in Greene's characters or themes; I find variety only in his brilliant inventiveness of incident, which seems to be inexhaustibly fertile. All Greene's novels are as subject to the tyranny of the last page as a railway train is subject to its destination. They lack autonomy. In Charles du Bos's words about a certain type of Catholic novelist, *"il se mue soi-même en un Deus ex machina."* I think the reason Mauriac never did this in his best work is that he retained his detachment towards his own church, and the only work of Greene's in which I wondered whether Greene might not be capable also of this detachment was that which pleased me least, his play *The Living Room,* where there were suggestions of impatience with Catholics' goodness, and piety, and pat answers. (The title could have a satirical ring if there had been any character in the play strong enough to represent a denunciation of those unco guid people who virtually smothered the unfortunate heroine to death by their appalling goodness.)

In his latest novel to date, *The Quiet American,* we see this habit of simplifying characters, in order to force them to illustrate a point, carried over to a story about a purely political problem. We are as oppressed as ever by a sense of inevitability. The character of the young American is so close to caricature that nothing but disaster can be expected from his ingenuous zeal; gradually we realize, in dismay, that the author has rigged the story in this way for the purposes of a political pamphlet very much as, earlier, he has rigged his stories to make a philosophical or theological observation. I find this particularly distressing in *The Quiet American.* After all, in the "religious" novels the theme, or point, was a general one. Here the point is particular, local and historical; we are, in fact, on the borders of the historical novel. If we lay the book to one side while reading it, to consider what our attitude would be to a novel about the theme of the "white man's burthen," or the theme of the

liberation of the Russian peasant by the Communist revolution, we will further realize that we are here on the
borders of the propagandist novel: for this young American
is not just any young foreigner anywhere — he is specifically
a representative figure in a given place at a given time. If
this be a just comment it follows that *The Quiet American*
is a novel in the class of *Uncle Tom's Cabin,* and is open to a
double form of criticism — literary and factual. Simplifica-
tion, or caricature, whether favorable or unfavorable, is
thereby a double fault. I could not, in reading this novel,
help thinking back several times to *For Whom the Bell
Tolls,* in which another American comes to Europe to take
part in another war, and on almost every count I found the
comparison between Hemingway's theme, indicated by the
title and the epigraph — generous, general and humane —
and Greene's misanthropy both informative and depressing.

I admit, gratefully and admiringly, that Graham Greene
has expanded our view of human nature by his constant
insistence on divine pity and divine mercy, and he must, in
doing this, have brought courage and consolation to a great
number of readers. It is hard to believe that the consolation
can outlive the discovery that he has not — outside that
triumphant book *The Power and the Glory* — wedded the
pity and the mercy to the complexity of our common day.
It is discouraging that in this latest novel, where the *deus
ex machina* is literally out of a machine, he has so little pity
of a purely human nature for human nature. "Thy will be
done in heaven as it cannot be on earth" is a prayer, and
an attitude, that leaves a novelist and his readers very little
breathing space or living room.

WILLIAM FAULKNER

More genius than talent

Every critic of Faulkner must be aware of the argument
put forward by certain of his admirers that he is not a novelist at all but a sort of prose poet. So Mr. Malcolm Cowley
writes: "Essentially he is not a novelist . . . he is an epic or
bardic poet in prose. . . ." I have assumed in the following
essay that Faulkner is a novelist, and wishes to be considered
as a novelist. Nothing I have read by any critic who has tried
to see the same writer both as a novelist and as a poet in the
same book, or who has tried to defend the alleged blending
of the two categories (as certain critics of Virginia Woolf
try to do), makes sense. It seems evident to me that what
Faulkner has tried to do is to write novels as I have earlier
defined a novel: that is, prose narratives dealing with a
number of characters whom he has tried to make both
persuasive and interesting, deployed in a manner which he,

*with his point of view, considers fitting, and which he hopes
to induce us to consider fitting also.*

*The basic assumption of the novel — call it what we will,
parable, allegory, legend — is that it is dealing with people
who are persuasive and interesting as recognizable fellow
beings. When a would-be novelist is described as a bardic
poet, he is being absolved from this limitation and is thereby
put outside the realm of criticism. In practice, Mr. Malcolm
Cowley inconsistently treats Faulkner as a novelist within
the definition I have given: as do all critics of Virginia
Woolf. Mr. Cowley's "Essentially he is not a novelist," etc.,
is merely a way of evading the admission that Faulkner —
like Mrs. Woolf — all too often tries to evade the inevitable
assumptions of this craft, or, for one reason or another, care-
lessly or willfully neglects them.*

NOT long ago I said to an intelligent critic of Joyce, "Tell
the truth! Do you not sometimes get utterly exasperated by him?" The critic smiled a slow smile and then
replied with disarming honesty, "As an avant-garde critic I
can never afford to be exasperated." I was so impressed by
this honest admission that it was not for several days after
that I realized how insulting to an author it is not to be
occasionally exasperated by him; for one presumes, re-
spectfully, that every author is being sincere, and if an
author is sincere he is almost certain to be exasperating at
some time or other. It is only the insincere authors who
are not exasperating: they are too smart for that. It is therefore a tribute to Faulkner to say that he is probably the most
exasperating author who ever deserved our respect.

It is always provoking when a writer has more genius

than talent. Sean O'Casey, with whom Faulkner might be compared, is this sort of writer. Gorki was another; so was Whitman. You never know what is going to come out of their mouths, golden wisdom or the most abysmal folly, and they least of all know it, because one of the great gifts that God gave them is their unself-consciousness. When they are really writing, that is, speaking out of their natural genius, the Holy Ghost talks through their mouths; when the divine current is not working they talk through their hats.

We are very familiar with this type of genius in Ireland, and from what little I have seen of Mississippi and all I have read about it, life there sounds very much like life in County Cork. There is the same passionate provincialism; the same local patriotism; the same southern nationalism — those long explicit speeches of Gavin Stevens in *Intruder in the Dust* might, *mutatis mutandis,* be uttered by a southern Irishman — the same feeling that whatever happens in Ballydehob or in Jefferson has never happened anywhere else before, and is more important than anything that happened in any period of history in any part of the cosmos; there is the same vanity of an old race; the same gnawing sense of old defeat; the same capacity for intense hatred; a good deal of the same harsh folk humor; the same acidity; the same oscillation between unbounded self-confidence and total despair; the same escape through sport and drink. There are, of course, differences. There is, for example, no escape in Ireland through sex. But there are enough similarities to make one sympathize profoundly with any writer born into such a community, and admire any writer who, as Faulkner has not been, is not silenced by the disadvantages of birth, education and tradition.

To read Faulkner is to invite a mixed and troubling pleasure. He is an ingenuous man, of strong feelings, a dedicated sincerity and poor equipment: a maimed genius. By no means the least of his handicaps — and from the point of view of mere pleasure as a "common reader" it is one of his greatest — is the fact that he cannot write plain English; not because he is untutored but because his psyche is completely out of his control. In this, again, he is strongly reminiscent of O'Casey. There are times when he seems to be writing with a blunt chisel on his grandfather's gravestone alone at midnight by candlelight; and times when he seems to be babbling into a microphone as if he were addressing a crowd of twenty thousand people. This creates a strong and often wholly justifiable temptation in the reader to cease to pay attention; thereby, it may be, losing some of Faulkner's best things when, quite without warning, the divine current is switched on again. The attentive listener nudges one awake with, "That was *good!*"; one pricks up one's ears; by the time one has caught Faulkner's drift once more, the divine current has probably been switched off again.

Another of his disconcerting ways is his weakness for picking up the bright tricks of other writers: for example, his willful, sporadic use of symbolism or his use of the famous Joyceian rhythms.*

---

* The Joyceian rhythms are various, but for the most part they are based on what one may call the reversed rhythm, of which the simplest example is (p. 43 of *Ulysses*): "The melon he had he held against my face." (It is reminiscent of the rhythm of Latin prose — *Melonem quem habuit contra faciem meam tenuit.* The references are to the Bodley Head edition of *Ulysses:* London, 1937.) The normal order of subject, verb, object is reversed or partly reversed. This, elaborated, gives us the rhythm of (p. 25): "His mother's prostrate body the fiery Columbanus in holy zeal bestrode"; instead of: "The fiery Columbanus bestrode his mother's prostrate body in

Now, no style, no influence, could be more alien to Faulkner's nature, which is wild-rushing and torrential, as his later books show; so that I feel it rather comical to come upon him shackling himself at the very beginning of his career, in *Soldier's Pay*, by such sentences as these: "Januarius Jones, baggy in gray tweed, being lately a fellow of Latin in a small college, leaned upon a gate of iron grillwork, breaking a levee of green and embryonically starred honeysuckle, watching April busy in a hyacinth dew." Or: "A branch dappled the rector's brow: a laureled Jove." Or: "Jones rose and under his eyes she walked mincing and graceful, theatrical with body-consciousness to the desk."

---

holy zeal." The intention is to place the emphasis less on the statement than on the visual image. So, again directing our attention to image rather than action (p. 33): "On his wise shoulders through the checkerwork of leaves the sun flung spangles, dancing coins." Or (p. 46): "Weary too in sight of lovers, lascivious men, a naked woman shining in her courts, she draws a toil of waters." This becomes infectious, urging a phrase to the foreground and then grudgingly yielding the verb, as in (p. 35): "Wombed in sin darkness I was too, made not begotten." (P. 35): "In a Greek watercloset he breathed his last." More elaborately (p. 40): "Lover for her love he prowled with Colonel Richard Burke, tanist of his sept, under the walls of Clerkenwell and, crouching, saw a flame of vengeance hurl them upward in the fog." The normal flow of sense being broken, the whole movement slows, until this reversed rhythm might be called a hesitation waltz: thus (p. 31): "Their eyes knew the years of wandering and, patient, knew the dishonours of their flesh." The ultimate so-called stream-of-consciousness style thus becomes an eddying, broken, halting stream, in slow motion, intellectually controlled, reined in firmly.

The verb, which, as we have seen, Joyce demotes in preference to the noun, finally tends either to hide away or vanish altogether or to decline into participles:

"On the steps of the Paris Stock Exchange the gold-skinned men quoting prices on their gemmed fingers. Gabbles of geese. They swarmed loud, uncouth about the temple, their heads thickplotting under maladroit silk hats. Not theirs: these clothes, this speech, these gestures. Their full, slow eyes belied the words, the gestures eager and unoffending, but knew the rancours massed about them and knew their zeal was vain. Vain patience to keep and hoard. Time surely would scatter all. A hoard heaped by the roadside: plundered and passing on. Their eyes knew the years of wandering and, patient, knew the dishonours of their flesh."

Or: "Sparse old silver on a buffet shadowed heavily under a high fanlight of colored glass, identical with the one above the entrance, her fragile white dress across the table from him: he could imagine her long subtle legs, like Atalanta's reft for running." One could find other instances from *Soldier's Pay* of this Joyceian influence.

He was still prone to literary kleptomania in his second novel, as three sentences from *Mosquitoes* show:

> Outside the window New Orleans, the vieux carré, brooded in a faintly tarnished languor like an ageing yet still beautiful courtesan in a smoke-filled room [*Yellow Book*], avid yet weary too of ardent ways. [*Joyce: Art thou not weary of ardent ways?*] Above the city summer was hushed into the bowled, weary passion of the sky. [*Omar Khayyam?*] Spring and the cruelest months [*Eliot*] were gone.

In *Pylon,* ten years after his first effort, he is still, as almost any dozen pages will show, writing under these influences. At the same time he is writing like this, from *Soldier's Pay:*

> The trumpets in his blood, the symphony of living, died away. The golden sand of hours bowled by day ran through the narrow neck of time into the corresponding globe of night, to be inverted and so flow back again. Jones felt the slow black sand of time marking his life away. "Hush," he said, "don't spoil it." The sentries in her blood lay down, but they lay down near the ramparts with the arms in their hands, waiting the alarm, the inevitable stand-to, and they sat clasped in the vaguely gleamed twilight of the room, Jones a fat Mirandola in a chaste Platonic nympholepsy, a religio-sentimental orgy in gray tweed, shaping an insincere, fleet-

ing articulation of damp clay to an old imperishable desire, building himself a papier-mâché Virgin.

Which is the onrushing way he really likes.

Then, there is his habit of writing in a variety of techniques. His first book, apart from the borrowed tricks to which I have referred, was entirely conventional. So is his second book, *Mosquitoes,* but it is quite different in its approach: it is intended to convey the impression that it was written by a sophisticated, urbane observer with a talent for reproducing or inventing brittle conversation. The change from *Mosquitoes* is total. In *Sartoris,* all pretensions to sophistication are dropped; he has become subjective, moody, oppressive, but the technique is the straightforward narrative of the normal historical novel. Then comes the highly self-conscious, intellectually conceived involution and incoherence of *The Sound and the Fury.* There is a direct break from all this in *As I Lay Dying,* which is clear-eyed, satirical, folksy and downright funny — I count it one of his best novels. Only in the excellent Snopes scenes is there any continuity between that fine novel and the facile, sexy thriller called *Sanctuary.* This is followed by the deeply felt and deeply moving blood-myth of *Light in August;* followed in turn by the feeble pseudomyth of *Pylon,* whose style is as embarrassing as it is exhausting. So he goes on, unpredictably. I cannot help recalling that splendidly vicious horse of Jewel Bundren's in *As I Lay Dying* which Jewel has to corral by swinging out of his nostrils, leaping on him like a hawk on the back of a crow, patting his neck with "short strokes, myriad and caressing," at the same time "cursing him with an obscene ferocity," dodging his wild

kick that makes a noise like a gunshot, stuffing the hay down
to him from the rack, saying, "Eat. Get the Goddam stuff out
of sight while you get the chance, you pussel-gutted bastard,
you sweet son of a bitch." Not being an avant-garde critic, I
can safely say that Faulkner's Pegasus has a lot of the in-
furiating qualities of this "pussel-gutted" animal.

But if we think him unpredictable we must first assure
ourselves that it is really he who encourages expectations
that he does not satisfy and not we who arouse them in ourselves. Consider, for example, the one major expectation
which most novel readers cherish but which he never did
anything to encourage, and which is capital to a critical as-
sessment of what he is really hoping to do. Most readers
nourish a very natural desire for the illusion of reality in fiction. Apart from the naturalism of his two first prentice novels, Faulkner never promised us this illusion, and with rare
exceptions he has never given it to us. There is always, as a
matter of course, a considerable element of what we call
realism in everything he writes, since it is impossible for
anybody to write a novel without some element of fidelity to
recognizable actualities; but such actualities are not his main
interest, and realism, contrary to popular belief, is not his
main technique.

Take the method of presentation used in his first characteristic novel, *Sartoris*. The last previous page he had written, the conclusion of *Soldier's Pay*, flows without a jolt into
the first pages of *Sartoris*. On that page, the parson and
Gilligan hear welling from within the Negroes' church "the
crooning, submerged passion of the dark race. . . . Then
the singing died, fading away along the mooned land inevitable with tomorrow and sweat, with sex and death and

damnation; and they turned townward under the moon feeling dust in their shoes." All Faulkner's characters have dust in their shoes from that on. It becomes a sandstorm in *Sartoris*, wherein Orpheus leads us so far underground at the first page that the story at once seems less a flower than a vegetable, or perhaps a fungus. The story, like its hero, young Bayard Sartoris, grows out of a cloud of memories as dusky as the inside of a mausoleum. Bayard comes out of an undefined past, evoking a darker and remoter past, with little promise of a future; and, as it transpires, he has no future except final failure and the release of death. The mood is necrolatrous and not for quite a while does it allow us to see even the bare outlines of the theme.

This word *theme* introduces a secondary critical problem, first raised, unwittingly, by Mr. Malcolm Cowley on the publication, in 1946, of his *Portable Faulkner*. It is sufficiently defined by the common use of the phrase "Yoknapatawpha Saga," as if over the intervening years Faulkner had organized his work into an American *Les Thibault*, a *Chroniques de Pasquier* or a *Forsyte Saga*. By 1946 Faulkner's novels were almost all out of print, and his reputation was not wide. Cowley's selection did a great deal to reawaken interest in Faulkner, but it did so in a special way: by choosing pieces which gave a false unity to Faulkner's work, pieces, that is, exclusively related to Yoknapatawpha County and to his history as a microcosm of the South. A great deal has since been written about this real or legendary county, and about Faulkner's treatment of it, but the fact is that one can read the individual novels without any such sense of total integration. So, when a popular (New American Library) edition of *Sartoris* tells us that "the spiraling descent of the Sartorises

[is] traced in the novel," it is simply not so; any more than that old Colonel Sartoris "dominates" the novel. It would be equally impossible for any reader to as much as get a hint from the novel of a social struggle between the family of Sartoris and Snopes: indeed, the Snopes family is only mentioned once in a single paragraph. Likewise, it is to read things into the novel to see any decline of traditional values in an alleged contrast between Aunt Jenny and Narcissa Benbow on the basis of Snopes's epistolary pursuit of Narcissa. Indeed, the whole of this part of the story is characteristically hazy, as if Faulkner only half understood what he or his characters are doing. When Snopes steals back his own letters, for instance, and Narcissa cannot remember whether or not she had destroyed them, one feels that one is dealing with a woman lost in a dream. Likewise, regarded as a document of Southern life, *Sartoris* is as unsatisfying as a portrait gallery visited by candlelight. Old Bayard had two sisters: we are told nothing whatever about them except the dates of their births. We can form no least image of Old Bayard's son, John, the father of young Bayard, the central figure of the novel. Virginia Sartoris's husband is a blank. The effect of such blanks, combined with the highly subjective method of presentation throughout, is obfuscatory. We have to read a hundred pages before we learn that young Bayard's wife was a Caroline White, that she died in childbirth in 1918, that the general date of the novel is 1919-1920. It is with some trouble that we fix in our minds the line of descent: John, Bayard, John, Bayard, John (or Johnny); so that it is a relief to find that the last-born Sartoris is not again Bayard but Benbow.

The presentation is equally obtuse. It is what the French

call *flou:* like a badly focused film. The central character, young Bayard, who gives his name to the title of the book, is a war-shattered aviator, a counterpart of the blinded and half-aware aviator of *Soldier's Pay.* The whole novel takes on something of his murkiness, his mental incoherence, the muzziness of a disintegrated nature shot to pieces by a sense of failure, guilt, confusion and incipient despair. He fills the air with dark intimations of mortality. He evokes repeatedly those abstractions that become so familiar to us in the later novels that one might call them Faulkner's boss words, *doom, doomed immortality, destiny, immortal doom, fatal, fatality, apotheosis* — "the stark dissolving apotheosis of his name" — life as an *illusion,* the image of men as *pawns* of God, or of circumstance, deprived of a personal will. Whenever Bayard is about, the mood of nature, in the full tradition of the pathetic fallacy, blends with his own moody sense of disintegration. So, when he comes back from hunting to his wife, wet to the skin, his lips cold on hers, his eyes bleak and haunted, "the trees gesture their black and sorrowful branches"; it is the season of "dissolution and death." When he is wandering in the woods in flight from his daemon, the baying of the hounds dies into echoes that repeat the sound, until its source is "lost and the very earth itself might have found voice grave and sad, and wild with all regret."

Now, Faulkner did not, I think, in the least intend this effect of a narcotic. It is clear that he originally planned the novel with more than adequate attention to actuality and then got lost in his own subjectivity. Without difficulty we can reconstruct in some detail the genealogical table of his preliminary notes, and in future editions of the novel this table might well be appended to the novel. So far as I have

been able to see, at no point within the novel does this plan
contradict itself, though he does contradict it in a couple of
details in later stories. We notice, too, that the soporific effect is often broken by passages and touches of the most intimately felt realism. He is always persuasive and detailed
when writing about dogs or hunting or Negroes. The possum
hunt in the middle of the book and Bayard's visit to the Negroes' cabin towards the end are photographically vivid. He
can be evocatively observant about very small things, intimate details of common life; as when we hear that Old
Bayard brings buttermilk in a thermos to the bank every
morning, drinks it at noon and sleeps for an hour after it; or
when we watch his dog regularly following his ritual move-
ments on his return home every afternoon. We feel suddenly
the heat and age of the little town on being told that the
gold lettering on the bank windows is "cracked." In *Light in
August* it is delightful to catch on the wing a reference to the
idlers sitting on the "heel-gnawed" steps of a country store.
The dog nosing in a cupboard has a "barometric tail"; the
dusty, hot air is "insect-rasped"; water adheres "in sliding
beads" to two freshly rinsed glasses; a coming frost will to-
night shrink the water in a pool about "rank bayonets of
dead grass in fixed glassy ripples in the brittle darkness"; on
a wet day the mournful sounds of the guns "linger in the
streaming air like a spreading stain"; when the sun is half
set behind hedges Bayard rides "stirrup-deep in cold air."
But my point is that these realistic details, which Turgenev
would have admired, are so few that if Faulkner does not accumulate them it can only be that he is not really interested
in them, or in naturalistic presentation at all.

This comparative indifference to, or even aversion for, an

actuality of detail which he is so well equipped to observe and utilize draws our attention back again, now with a new understanding, to the effect of the novel as a whole: to its subjectivity, to its vague, self-confused, irresolute characters (the only character who has a will of her own is Aunt Jenny), its pervasive sense of all-dominating fate — on the very last pages he calls his characters "pawns, shaped too late and to an old, dead pattern, and of which the Player Himself is a little weary" — until we realize that this is a writer who is not primarily interested in human beings for their own sakes. If we agree that a writer does not coldly select his characters and subjects but is chosen by them, that they are compulsions of his nature, we cannot but feel that Faulkner is himself involved in the incoherence, haziness and irresolution of his characters, that they are reflections of himself. One begins to tremble for a writer so gravely handicapped.

I am sensitively aware that this is not the usual view taken of Faulkner's methods. It is more generally assumed that he writes as he does because he chooses to write that way. If one were at any point entirely satisfied that he was getting as close to his own purpose as he wished to get, this assumption would not be, as I think it is, an abnegation of the function of criticism. But one gets no such sense of security from his work: least of all from his groping style. Those sequences of possible words — "it was seeking, hunting . . ."; "he had invented, made it . . ."; "He would never have said this, put it into words himself . . ." — suggest only a man who does not know what he is about to say. So does the use of second-thought words: "He did not know why he had been compelled, or anyway needed, to claim it . . ."; "This, anyway, will, shall, must be invulnerable . . ."; "He kept the style pure and intact and unchanged and inviolate . . ."; "a willingness to surrender, relinquish himself . . ." Most disconcerting is his way of saying "I mean," whose corollary is that he often does not know what he means. The fustian language he uses is of the same order and origin. He is a writer not swimming along on the river of his intention but drowning in it. So, when he writes about "the gasoline-roar of apotheosis" he is relying on sound rather than sense. It is a common romantic habit. Is he using, with care, the artist's meaningful language or the demagogue's careless, rhetorical and often meaningless language when he writes of an "unbelievable quantity" or of an "incredible height"? The sounds of words intoxicate him. "A thunderous and silent solitude." "The oblivious and arch-adultress." "The apotheosis of his youth assumed a thousand avatars." I must, however, insist that my purpose here is not to find fault with Faulkner for using this type of English — though I think it tedious, ineffective and, at times, bogus. My point is single — to draw attention to the dissociation from what, for short, we may here call common realities; indicated by this romantic style. It is an outward mark of an inward failure to focus clearly.

Pylon is an outstanding example of lack of focus. The characters in this novel move like shadows through shadows, and this is true not only of the drunks — in whose case it would be understandable — but of all the characters. Now, it was particularly necessary that this should not happen in this book. If a writer is describing a fog he himself must not be fogged; if he is treading his way through a jungle he, at least, must have a map; if he is dealing with extraordinary events he must work doubly hard to make them credible. In all his work I have come on no scene more unpersuasive than the fantastic description of how the pilot Shuman copulates acrobatically with Laverne, in the cockpit of his plane while stunting thousands of feet above a crowd, just before she parachutes.

This regrettable scene could be comic. It is patently being presented as a scene of "great strength." The sequel is even more extraordinary. When Laverne sails to the ground, her clothes are blown away from her naked body. One of the officials goes berserk with lust and chases her. If one's sense of humor were raw enough, or strong enough, to see the fun in lust — which is, indeed, at times extravagantly absurd — one might, again, take this scene as a comic scene, or as, at least, intended to be a comic scene; but there is nothing in the style of the whole section to suggest that Faulkner was himself amused. The only comic thing in the section is the fustian grandeur of the English. One is driven to conclude that in these odd pages we are very close to delirium; and this not because the author has chosen to deal with moon-struck characters — why should he not do so? — or because the moon-struck characters seem to have taken possession of the author and made him their slave; but that Malraux was right when he said that Faulkner conceives his situations in the void without thinking of characters at all. He preimagines, says Malraux, *l'écrasement des personnages inconnus.* Here we ask ourselves: whence does this concept of *écrasement* come? If a novelist begins not with people but with situations peopled only by faceless ghosts, will he be able to hold his grip on empirical reality? And how can we refer back from his imaginative excitement, coruscating in the stratosphere of an unpopulated void, to any kind of living norm? The fact is that we often cannot.

The only explanation I can offer for Faulkner's frequent factual inaccuracies and contradictions, which many critics have noted but which they have usually dismissed indulgently without comment, is this same alienation or mental dissociation from common reality. Of these *The Wild Palms* offers a striking illustration. (It also fits in neatly with Malraux's idea — expanded further by Magny in her *L'Âge du Roman Américain* — that the psychological characteristics of Faulkner's personages are strictly predetermined by the necessities of his mechanical concept of man. But this is, of course, not peculiar to Faulkner: it is the common mark of the naturalistic novel, which is always based on a determinist philosophy.) In *The Wild Palms* the key incident is a bungled abortion. To quote Mlle. Magny, who has also noted the mechanistic influence: "The character of the doctor (Harry Wilbourne), of Charlotte (his mistress), the various circumstances of the life they share are all ordained by this failure; the elements of their lives and characters have no other reality, no other function except in so far as they converge on this inevitable catastrophe." Now, this being so, it is obvious that the circumstances of the abortion should have been plotted with extreme care. What happens, we will recall, is that Harry bungles the abortion of his mistress's child not through incapacity or through ignorance — he has previously performed an abortion with complete success — but because, owing to strong feelings of moral delicacy, certain natural inhibitions and a proper professional distaste, he keeps on postponing the operation until it is too late for safety. His character is well built up on those lines and his indecisiveness is emphasized. Unfortunately, we find if we correlate the dates given in the course of the novel that, in fact,

Faulkner is so careless about his mechanism that it is he who bungles. Wilbourne does not delay the operation more than at most two weeks beyond two months; and, as we know, abortions can safely be performed far later than this. All we are left with as a result of Faulkner's carelessness about the dates is that the tragedy was an accident: this, obviously, cools off the whole point of the story. We can only conclude that Faulkner was not sufficiently interested in the essential realities of the narrative to give them his full attention. It is the over-all impression his work leaves on the reader. He lets his imagination run away with, or from, reality.*

* The essential sequence of dates in *The Wild Palms* is as follows: While in Chicago, three weeks after Christmas Harry gets a post in Utah, leaves two mornings later, and so arrives, we presume, around January 20. *"They had been there a month, it was almost March now"* brings us to about February 20. Three days later the Buckners leave: before they leave Harry performs a successful abortion on Mrs. Buckner. It is on the night of their departure that Charlotte conceives, as she duly reveals to Harry later, explaining that it had been too cold for her to get out of bed again for the douche. This night, the key date, must be in or before the last week in February.

Later, at an unspecified date, Charlotte returns home to see her children; as Harry waits for her in a park he recalls that it was *"not five months ago"* since they left Chicago for Utah, which, on referring back, would put this date in the park somewhere in mid-June. Actually, however, we are told a little farther on that it is now *"not yet June."* This obliges us to fix the date of the scene in the park, and of Charlotte's return to her husband's home, after May 20 (any earlier it would be only four months since they left Chicago for Utah) and before May 31: *"not yet June."* During her meeting with her husband Charlotte says the abortion took place *"a month ago";* which fixes the date of the bungled abortion as being somewhere between the twentieth, and the thirtieth of April. Therefore the abortion was not delayed unduly. Everything in the character of Harry Wilbourne which had been built up on the idea that it had been falls to pieces.

Also, it may be noted that when Charlotte is pleading with Harry to perform the abortion she points out to him wildly that in thirteen days four months will have passed. It is not clear what she means by this — either four months since she conceived, or four months after she missed her first menstrual period after conception. In either case we were *there* led to believe that Harry performed the abortion after June 20. The contradictions are apparent.

Were he to hear himself spoken of in these terms he would probably be amused, for he doubtless — it seems plain from his work — thinks himself a realist. In fact he has taken the determinism of the naturalist technique and philosophy to its logical absurdity, which is the kind of splendidly honest folly we might, a priori, expect from his intense but fundamentally simple nature. Absolute naturalism cannot, of its determinist nature, present a coherent record of anything except a machine. And this, in effect, is what Sartre has said in the most penetrating thing so far written about Faulkner.* His metaphysic of time, Sartre points out, involves the denial of the future in so far as it is a denial of a free present. What we call the present is to Faulkner embedded in *and controlled by* an undefined, indefinable and unending continuum which bears no relation to what we call chronological time. What we call the present and future, all that moves towards the future willfully, is to him a continuation of timeless fate. He has, in short, drowned himself and all humanity in timelessness. Human potency is castrated. In our sense nothing ever happens: it merely recurs. He has, whether he knows it or not, thereby killed the human will.

Tied up with all this is Faulkner's concept of memory. It is not a power which orders the past. It is an incoherent thing, more in the nature of a trancelike obsession induced

---

I have yet to meet an American student of Faulkner who does not consider *The Wild Palms* a very fine and moving love story. This should not encourage any reader of these pages to think that Americans are indifferent to actuality in literature: it is, rather, part of the attitude which regards Faulkner not as a novelist but as a sort of lyric poet or myth maker to whom the greatest degree of "poetic license" must be allowed. It is the only possible attitude which absolves him from normal criticism.

*See *William Faulkner,* edited by Frederick J. Hoffman and Olga W. Vickery, Michigan State College Press, 1951, pp. 180 ff.

by recurrences. Compare his "memories" with Proust's illuminating "essences." Proust nourished a delicate idealism in his search for mortal immortality, surmounting reality and its inevitable corruption. His search for "lost" time found a refined Being within us which "can only be nourished on the essence of things and finds in them alone its subsistence and delight." He nevertheless fashions his magic out of reality by a perpetual sensibility to all its physical details. Nor does Proust, as Claude-Edmonde Magny points out, deride even that intelligence which is the enemy of the "real impression" — as opposed to the images of what produced it, images which are too visual, too fleshy to be "essences." He says explicitly:

> Certainly we are obliged to relive our particular suffering with the courage of a physician who tries over again upon himself an experiment with a dangerous serum. But we ought to think of it under a general form which enables us to some extent to escape from its control by making all men co-partners in our sorrow, and this is not devoid of a certain gratification. Where life closes round us, intelligence pierces an egress. . . . The intellect does not recognise situations in life which have no issue. (*Des situations fermées de la vie sans issue.*)

He invites us likewise to free ourselves by a similar meditation. Nothing could be farther from the epileptic trances and daemonic possessions of Faulkner in which all reality explodes or evaporates before our *unintelligent* eyes.

If we accept this Faulknerian antagonism to time and free action a great deal in his work at once becomes clear. Logically, he should, as part of the general impotence of humanity, not write at all; logically, he should find nothing much worth writing about. But write he must since he is a writer, and anyway his metaphysic is untenable in practice, and nobody of larger stature than a jellyfish could live according to it. What we are therefore to observe is a man struggling in the meshes of his own self-created dilemma and finding chiefly three ways out of his dilemma.

The first escape is to contradict himself by permitting the occasional upsurgence of will — all those brave and gallant Civil War scenes; though we note that his heroes are few, and mostly fated to destruction and failure. The second and more logical escape is to see men not as men but as an abstraction or myth called man. The third is laughter, and is his best escape of all.

Certain habits in his writing now become more understandable; especially his general air of incoherence and fogginess — for who, with so nihilistic a view of human life, can be interested in depicting its actualities in loving detail? We can understand his love for these familiar boss words, of which, I suggest, the most illuminating is the word *avatar*, which he uses over and over again, implying perpetual reincarnation. We can understand his attraction for idiots, "feebs" and subhumans, who represent life without hope, direction or intelligence. So with his escape via brutality; via his obsession with animal sex, to us base, comic or absurd, to him at once normal in man, and a crude release for that dammed-up energy which, in another writer, would express itself in scenes of creative thought or action; via his use of the castration symbol, the stallion symbol, the myth of blood and soil; and, at his best, via his satirical humor.

His first escape from his own logic — contradiction — was inevitable. Sartre calls him, in one place, a lost man; and in another, a mystic. He is both: *une âme damnée*. For, as Sartre says, "mystical ecstasies are our only means of escaping from the temporal world" — what the common reader might call common reality — "and a mystic is always a man who wants to forget something: his self or, more generally, language or formal representation." But mystics generally deny this life because of their greater interest in another life. Faulkner does not apparently share this common mystical hope, and so he is, indeed, in cursing the only world he knows, a loser. Side by side, for excellence, with Sartre's essay I would put Mr. Arthos's illuminating essay on Faulkner — *Ritual and Humour* — an examination of his third form of escape from the closed ring he has built about himself, the escape of laughter. But before dealing with this, Mr. Arthos makes two very illuminating remarks. He points out that if we are, as Faulkner feels, cursed, "there must have been some initial evil, some original deviation from our nature"; which forcibly reminds me of John Henry Newman's frightened realization (a man also very conscious of evil) that "the whole human race must have been implicated in some terrible original calamity": a calamity which he, in the terminology of Christian mythology, would, of course, call Original Sin, its horror evaded by the beautiful story of a young god descending on earth to expiate it. Faulkner, however, Mr. Arthos points out, has no such ontology (he calls it "theology"), and in its absence seems to be conscious that he has been constructing a pseudodemonology. This, I think, is very much what Sartre means by saying that Faulkner, being lost, and knowing it, pushes his logic to the fatal end. It is, I think, very much what Baudelaire meant when he said in *Les Paradis Artificiels,* "In sum, man is forbidden under pain of intellectual suicide [*déchéance et mort*] . . . so to alter his destiny as to substitute for it a fate of another order. Every man who refuses to accept the conditions of life sells his soul." (*Tout homme qui n'accepte pas les conditions de la vie vend son âme.*) Sooner or later this would have to dawn on Faulkner. When it does he must realize that he cannot stick to his early premises. He would have to break out of his own jail.

It is precisely because Faulkner has pushed his philosophy to its logical limits in *The Sound and the Fury* that it is such an interesting — as it is a unique — literary experiment. Let us recall it as a test case.

The novel deals with the Compson family. Caroline Bascomb, who dies, somewhat unconventionally, four years after the novel is completed, had married one Jason Compson, equally addicted to rye and to the classics. She is a widow. They have had four children: in order of age, Quentin, born in 1890; Candace, born in 1892; Jason, born, or so one reconstructs, in 1894; and Benjamin, born in 1895, gelded in 1913, committed to the lunatic asylum in 1933 and still living. Candace, a wild girl between the ages of fifteen and seventeen, married when eighteen an Indianian named Sidney Herbert Head, on April 25, 1910, being then pregnant for two months with a female child, later called Quentin, of doubtful parentage — she may be the daughter of one Gerald Bland or, more likely, of one Dalton Ames. Candace is cast off by Head in 1911, possibly — no other reason is suggested — because he realizes that the child is not his.

All this, however, is painful and uncertain reconstruction, and some of the dates do not click persuasively. For if the girl Quentin was, as we gather, conceived in February

1910, the child would have been born in November 1910; and though admittedly a seven-month baby, this premature birth was not total evidence of premarital infidelity. (Possibly, as usual, Faulkner has not worked it out carefully.) I may say that this girl Quentin's age is given as being "at seventeen" in April 1928, whereas she must actually have been seventeen in November 1927. We are told (in an appendix) that Candace then brought her child home and returned no more. This is also contradicted by the novel, where she returns not once but several times. (Modern Library edition; pages 220, 224, 228.) In any case we are also told in the novel that it was her father who brought the child home (page 215). For a number of years, variously given as seventeen and eighteen, she pays her brother Jason two hundred dollars a month to keep the child, because Jason is not wealthy. He is described in the Appendix as having started his own business at the age of thirty. It has to be noted, however, that he is clearly depicted in the novel as being an employee. Jason's age introduces another factual difficulty. We can fix his birth at 1894. It is a little puzzling that, as Benjy's guardian, he has the boy castrated in 1913, since the guardian was himself then only nineteen! We are told (in the Appendix) that Quentin commits suicide on June 2, 1910, though I confess, as a reader of normal vigilance, that if I had not been told so (by the Appendix) I should not have observed it on reading this section of the novel. Such is the family and their story, extracted from some typical Faulknerian contradictions.

We know the peculiar way in which the author unfolds the story. Both of the first two sections are obscure. The first is an interweaving of past and present as seen mainly through the mind of an idiot. The second goes back to a date eighteen years earlier and is seen through the mind of a neurotic on the point of committing suicide. The third comes forward again and enters into objectivity, to show us Uncle Jason and his niece, the girl Quentin, in conflict. And the events of the fourth section, dated two days later, are seen partly through the eyes of the Negro servants and partly through Jason's. Omitting the Quentin flash back, the sequence of days is the Saturday, then the Friday, then the Sunday of Holy Week.

Any value this treatment could have experimentally would depend on its being willed, consistent and successful. It is none of these three things. Why then did he write his book in this tortured fashion? Having imprisoned himself and his characters in a will-less world where all action is fated, whose occupants, like all "lifers," are limited to thought, memory, routine, perhaps to despair, he had to write strabismally, his refracted vision* matching the torture of their frustrating situation. The treatment of the first two sections is logically of that order. But the metaphysic begins to break down in section three. There the ambitious and resolute Jason enters in; and while there is, or may be, a suggestion that nothing he can do about young Quentin will avert fate, are we, when we see him attending to his private af-

---

* Sartre's clear-headed statement on Faulkner's "vision" (*loc. cit.*) puts this better than anybody else has done: "Nothing happens, the story does not progress; rather, we discover it behind each word as an oppressive and hateful presence, varying in intensity with each situation. It is a mistake to think of these anomalies as mere exercises in virtuosity; the novelist's aesthetic always sends us back to his metaphysic. The critic's task is to bring out the author's metaphysic before evaluating his technique. And it is obvious that Faulkner's is a metaphysic of time." He then goes on to define this metaphysic of the will-castrated Time concept, or obsession, which dominates this writer.

fairs, his investments, for example, to presume that these also are the toys of fate? In the last section there is a revealing sentence about Jason which seems to intimate that the author cannot hold on any longer to the idea of a will-less humanity. This occurs when Jason, chasing after his sister, who has robbed him, pauses to plan his line of action: "He could see the opposed forces of his destiny and his will drawing swiftly together now, toward a junction that would be irrevocable; he became cunning. I can't make a blunder, he told himself. There would be just one right thing, without alternatives: he must do that." It is a sentence which reveals clearly the presence of both ambiguity and strain in the double concept of destiny and autonomy (will).

The Sound and the Fury raises, also, the matter of Faulkner's sporadic and capricious use of symbolism. It is more than a minor irritation. For, unless a writer use his symbolism consistently, and unless it is clear that a symbolic way of speech is an indispensable part not only of his technique but of his nature, the reader must feel that it may be safely ignored. So, when we first take up *The Sound and the Fury* our attention is naturally attracted to the insistence on the paschal time, on observing that the first, third and fourth of the four chapters of the book occur on the Saturday, Friday and Sunday of Holy Week in the year 1928. But what has happened to the Thursday? Where there is so much insistence on dates they must, we feel, mean something. We note that the second chapter is dated June 2, 1910. Hopefully we remember that Corpus Christi commemorates the establishment of the Christian Pasch, or Eucharist, and was transferred in the Middle Ages from the Thursday of Holy Week to its present position in the liturgical year, two months after

Easter. Hopefully we examine the calendar. Alas, June 2, 1910, was not Corpus Christi. The date has no symbolical significance whatever. Again, since so much happens in Holy Week, on these three April dates, and since the theme emphasizes *a recurrent pattern* in the lives of the Compsons, our attention is naturally arrested when we are explicitly told that Candace Compson married Sidney Herbert Head on April 25, 1910, two months before her big brother Quentin committed suicide. Again we examine the calendar, reasonably expecting to find that Faulkner will have selected another Easter date. But in 1910 Easter did not fall on April 25. Once more a pointless date. Or, again, when we go through the Easter liturgy, so rich in symbol and imagery, we fail to come on any sign that Faulkner has been there before us, as Joyce would indubitably have been in a like circumstance.

A few such experiences in chase of these symbolic hares — the Joe Christmas name in *Light in August* is another fair example — not unnaturally lead us to believe that his use of symbol is entirely capricious, and probably not so much literary as therapeutic: that is to say, he has found it a helpful occasional stimulant.

It might be added that some critics, at least, who have concentrated on Faulkner's alleged symbolism do not inspire any greater confidence: as when Mr. Richard Chase, writing of *Light in August* in the *Kenyon Review* in the autumn of 1948, said:

> The word "burden" seems to have the same significance for the Southern writers as the pack of the peddler had for Hawthorne and Melville: the "burden" of one's history or of one's continually self-annihilating humanity. Miss Burden, in

Light in August, is not the only character in Southern fiction so named.

It is an approach which opens up tempting possibilities, ranging from the symbolic sense of Jason to the phallic possibilities of Hightower or Bunch; nor will the careful student ignore the symbolical significance of the name Chase; nor fail to remember, when Bayard Sartoris kisses Drusilla Hawk in "An Odor of Verbena" from *The Unvanquished,* that the German for hawk is *Falke,* which suggests clearly that Faulkner must have had incestuous relations with his own great-grandmother. It is the same Mr. Chase who has discovered linear and curvular symbolisms in *Light in August* and a special significance in the fact that Mrs. McEachern washes the feet of Joe Christmas — given as a transpicuously clear reference to the fact that Christ washed the feet of the disciples — and that Joe Christmas's women are always trying to feed him, including, of all unlikely women, a waitress. The common reader will not be unwise to remember Jowett of Balliol's remark about a certain learned German's critical methods: that such methods obscure rather than illuminate and pile up mountains of chaff when there is no more wheat — and skip lightly over Faulkner's actual or alleged symbolism.

As to the success of the experiment of *The Sound and the Fury,* even if no avant-garde critic dare admit that as a novel it fails disastrously, I think that even the most *avant* of avant-garde critics will have to agree that it is so unreadable, in that complete sense of the word *read* which implies to understand, that it might be safely wagered that nobody on earth ever has read or ever will read the novel except Faulkner himself.

Nevertheless, though not an admirable novel, it is an admirable performance. Houdini has escaped his bonds. Faulkner should, by all the laws of his attitude to life, have been silenced. He has not been silenced. He has found one of two ways of speaking out, if not very clearly. Either he is saying, "Granted my premise, this is the way human beings act in real life"; or he is saying, "I am not describing real life and actual human beings. I am writing an allegory of my own feelings about life, my ideas, myself. I am giving you not a novel but a fantasy with the effect of a parable."

I would define it in this latter way, and I suggest that much, if not most, of Faulkner's work is likewise in the region of fantasy, with or without the effect of parable. This also, I suggest, is how the common reader reads him, granting him his premises for the purpose of the argument; that is, granting him what I. A. Richards calls emotional belief as against intellectual assent, very much as we give temporary assent to the premises of a poem about the Last Judgment when we do not believe that there is or will be any such thing as a Last Judgment. The reader is impressed, puts the books away, and thereafter remembers them not as books but as a man. In the words of a popular advertisement for petrol, he says, "That's Faulkner, that was." As if he had seen a falling star. I may add, having tested it over and over again, that most readers of Faulkner other than academes possess only a very limited knowledge of his work.

So much for the bonds of logic and escape from them — however partial and unsatisfactory — through self-contradiction. He could not have gone very far in this way, nor did he try to. We may pass over the sexy *Sanctuary:* escape from silence (*le vertige de la page blanche*) through crude violence is the commonest form of pseudoliberation. In *Light in August* we find that he has paused to take stock of his problem again, and this time he surmounts it magnificently. He does it by going back behind his anger, misery and consequent nihilism to primal causes expressed in the form of a myth big enough to justify them.

It is true that his first impulse may have been, probably was, in the actual world: that he heard about an old local scandal, or had seen a house on fire, or an old shell of a ruined home deep in weeds, and began to reconnoiter the lives that lay behind; and the success of the novel is partly due to the fact that if the reader so wishes he may find adequate reward in this reconstruction alone. But if he is a more demanding reader he will find behind the reality, as Faulkner himself did, something much more impressive, what, for short, we call a theme, or that essential of all fiction which is not merely entertainment, a *manière de voir*.

As for the human interest, the scaffolding has here been carefully constructed beforehand, and it can be reconstructed with only a little difficulty. Calvin Burden, a high-spirited, idealistic Northern abolitionist, settled after the Civil War in the South, has among other children a son Nathaniel, born in 1836. Nat is a wanderer. He marries a Mexican-Spanish woman named Joanna in 1852 or 1853, who bears him a son, young Calvin, born in 1854. Both Calvins, grandfather and grandson, are shot by one Colonel Sartoris in 1874. Nathaniel then marries, in 1886, aged fifty, a New Englander, who bears him a daughter, Joanna, in 1888. So much for the past, here fully creative and relevant. This Joanna Burden now lives alone in an old house near Jefferson, doing good among the Negroes. She is an upright,

self-sacrificing, devoted humanitarian, at first disliked by her
neighbors, but, by the time she has reached forty, accepted
as an oddity or an aberrant. She is the pivot of the story. Into
her lonely and virtuous life, at the age of forty, there comes
a white-skinned mulatto named Joe Christmas, aged thirty,
a bastard orphan brought up by a dour couple who had
taken him out of the orphanage and adopted him, but
treated him so severely that his hand is now turned against
all mankind. His mixed blood has, in any case, fissurated
him so terribly since childhood that he hardly knows whether
he hates the whites or the Negroes the more. He carries in
his blood the invisible mark of Cain. He seduces the forty-
year-old Joanna, corrupts her almost to the point of insanity,
and finding that she wants to marry him, reform him and,
what is entirely unbearable, that she wants to make of him
a protector of the Negroes — that is, she would make him
the prisoner of his own black blood — he murders her sav-
agely. He flees, is taken, and is shot. Out of evil (slavery)
cometh good (Joanna). Out of good cometh evil (Joe Christmas).

As in *The Sound and the Fury,* the critical events of the
novel are all compressed into a short span of time. They oc-
cupy less than a single month: the August of 1931. In that
month we begin to read Joanna Burden's tragic story at its
tragic conclusion, at the moment when Lena Grove, a girl
from farther north who had been seduced by a worthless fellow named Lucas Birch and has been traveling southward in
search of him, approaches the town of Jefferson just when
Joanna's house is on fire. (Her murderer had set it on fire
the night before.) The twin story of Joanna Burden and Joe
Christmas rises in eddies like the smoke of that fire, casts its

smell and fumes over the whole countryside, reveals itself bit by bit as smoke reveals its source in a shifting wind. Two other characters act as the clearing wind: one Byron Bunch, who befriends Lena, and a retired parson, Hightower. Both of them are rather shadowy characters and are possibly invented as two good men to offset the two bad men of the story. Towards the end two more characters enter, the Hyneses, father and mother of Milly Hynes, the mother of Joe Christmas — old Hynes thirsting melodramatically for the death of Christmas, his wife anxious to save him. About three weeks after she first appeared on the road south, Lena Grove has her baby and takes again to the road, now accompanied by Byron Bunch. So the story closes as it began. It is, all in all, a finely wrought and well-constructed novel.

We now come to the second, or thematic, interest. The underlying myth is as old as Genesis, that anthology of primal curses: of Adam, and Cain, and Hagar, and Sodom. The myth which Faulkner chose to express Newman's "aboriginal calamity" was that of Babel, felt not in terms of language but of race or blood. The doom inherent in this fatality of birth makes Negro blood and white blood destroy one another, not merely in terms of South and North, but of a mutual, inescapable, personal, archetypal corruption. Joanna's pity for the Negroes corrupts itself by her lust for the mulatto. The two mingled bloods in the mulatto destroy them both. There can be few scenes in literature so horrible as the collapse of Joanna Burden. The sexual excesses of this good middle-aged woman, running naked through her parson father's house, hiding naked in cupboards for the mulatto to find her, strewing herself under bushes in the dark for him to smell her out, are like the cackle of demons at the

futility of all human effort to breed goodness out of an aboriginal evil. Before that central tragedy the many weaknesses in the novel are forgiven: the cardboard figures of
Hightower and Byron Bunch, the exaggerated caricatures of
McEachern or of Hynes; the whole phantomlike quality of
both Joanna and Christmas, which increases as the myth becomes more and more insistent. In the shadow of the dark
myth which Faulkner has evoked it seems right that men
and women should present themselves to us as Breughel-
esque phantoms and grotesques, as giants and dwarfs, not
as human beings of normal experience.

We begin, at last, to see why it is inherent in Faulkner's
method that his characters should always be now gigantic,
now manikin size, alternately enlarged and diminished by
association with, identification with or subjection to forces
greater than themselves.

Here, from *Intruder in the Dust*, in his most barbaric sort
of English, is a simple example of man reduced to manikin:

> . . . his uncle came through the door and drew it after
> him, the heavy steel plunger crashing into its steel groove
> with a thick oily sound of irrefutable finality like that ulti-
> mate cosmolined doom itself when as his uncle said man's
> machines had at last effaced and obliterated him from the
> earth and, purposeless now to themselves with nothing left
> to destroy, closed the last carborundum-grooved door upon
> their own progenitorless apotheosis behind one clockless
> lock responsive only to the last stroke of eternity.

Or here is another example of a human being reduced to
insignificance. It occurs farther on, in the same novel. The
boy is hoping that he and his companions will do what they
have to do in time to help the Negro Lucas Beauchamp; but

even as he hopes, he does not dare to articulate the hope —
"because thinking it into words even only to himself was like
the struck match which doesn't dispel the dark but only exposes its terror, one weak flash and glare revealing for a second the empty roads, the dark and empty land's irrevocable,
immitigable negation." The same concept is defined, quite
explicitly, in Gavin Stevens's long monologue wherein we
are bidden to see each unique man being formed by

> the dirt, the earth, which had bred his bones and those of
> his fathers for six generations, and which was still shaping
> him into not just a man but a specific man, not with just a
> man's passions and aspirations and beliefs but the specific
> passions and hopes and convictions and ways of thinking and
> acting of a specific kind and even race . . .

There it seems at first that we are to think of Southern nationalism as an emotional idea atavistically powerful to mold
men into a homogeneous form; as when we are told that
"only a few of us know that from homogeneity comes anything of a people or for a people of lasting value . . . a national character." But before Stevens concludes his speech
the threnody swells into the idea that "man's immortality is
in the suffering he has endured, his struggle towards the
stars in the steppingstones of his expiations," and we realize that what Faulkner is creating is a sort of anonymous
man, a faceless type of all mankind.

This idea is specifically stated by the boy himself, who
says he wishes his deed to be anonymous, unpraised, "want-
ing nothing except his own one anonymous chance to perform something brave and passionate and austere not just in
but into man's enduring chronicle . . . to be found worthy
to present" (with his people) "one united front to the dark

abyss the night." Even more specifically still, Stevens states the same idea when he explains how man becomes mob, which becomes mass, which becomes so large that it becomes man again, capable of pity, capable of longing for "the one serene universal light," through his belief in "more than the divinity of individual man (which we in America have debased into a national religion . . .) but in the divinity of his continuity as Man." Man — with, we note, the abstraction of the capital letter. In the light of this it is no wonder that it has been asked whether what Faulkner has written are novels or a series of moralizations, disguised as fiction, about the perpetually embryonic plasma of a never-to-be-born abstraction.

One thing is clear. That Faulkner at any time made a clear decision to accept the simple realities of his countryside and write a saga about them is not true. But he has made that essential adjustment occasionally, sporadically, and whenever he has employed the third and most successful solution of all for his dilemma: whenever, that is, he has looked at life with humor. It is strange that he had not come sooner on this dissolvent of tragedy, for the Negroes had come upon it long before him. They had been more wise than he, more civilized in the sense of being more life-clever, better artists even in their folklore and folk songs. For much of what he has written is a crude, barbaric yawp, and nothing that they created out of an actual physical misery far greater than his subjective misery is as barbaric or as crude as much of what he has done. But, then, the Negroes have something that Faulkner has thrown away or never had: they really are an integral race, though, like the Jews, a race without a nation, and they have what he never had or threw away, a real sense of homogeneity. All that is best in Faulkner came from his closeness of feeling for the Negro — such as *Light in August,* or *Intruder in the Dust.* Ishmael learning from Ishmael. He has written best of all when he has written like a Negro, in the folk-humorous vein of *As I Lay Dying.* That novel is written by a slave breaking free with laughter: bitter, cruel, rank laughter, but much more effective than his angers and his protestations, because, quite simply, it is true to common experience. It is the sort of humor, made out of misfortune, that recalls Figaro's famous answer to Almaviva's question as to where he got his philosophy: *"L'habitude du malheur!"* It is humor learned from misfortune, and conquering it.

Place has been, in this sense, *the* capital influence on Faulkner as writer. The Negro's lot has illuminated his concept of man, yet at the same time darkened it. So might a young South African be stirred awake to human values, yet confused and divided also. This catalyst has produced a change, unchanging itself, unaffected by him whom it changes; its unchangeability, its exasperation, its timelessness are overpowering. More, it signifies frustratingly what it does not adequately symbolize, the dignity of man. Those black signposts, unreadable, confuse, yet point onward. But the subject is inadequate for humanist treatment. These characters whose abused humanity appeals to Faulkner so strongly are less than human because they are abused. He, the white, cannot find enough riches here to satisfy his own needs. He therefore has to inflate his themes. This common reality will not stand prolonged examination on the basis of its common reality. Hence his symbolism, his extravagance, his surges of orgiastic emotionalism. Reality (he feels) fails him, lets him down. His realism is therefore a *faux réalisme.*

It is inflated in its anger and its excitement. It is a form of realism like Zola's, sodden with romanticism and self-pity, expressive chiefly of some unsatisfied hunger, like a sexual hunger. It is at its best a howl of protest, negative in answer to negations, altogether a personal despair and a personal frustration. The frustrated characters are projections of his own defeat.

What attracts one in Faulkner is that he has always been "game." He has felt an urge of passion, of pity, towards, one feels, some ideal that he cannot define. One responds with admiration tinged with an affectionate pity that surmounts one's exasperation at the sort of performance he puts up. It is like watching a boxer who is full of spirit but who has no skill, so that one can hardly bear to watch him being mauled. He is at his best when he is laughing, with a face cut to bits and one eye shut. One knows very well that the fight is uneven and why it is uneven. There is no way, for him, of controlling cause and effect inside the old traditional order of values, and he has not enough intellectual equipment either to express his own ideas while utilizing the images of traditional society — as Gide, or Elizabeth Bowen, or Virginia Woolf, or even the rebellious Hemingway, has done — or to surmount that traditional structure imaginatively as Lawrence did. Everything he writes is written as an angry, passionate, generous, fumbling, rebellious, bewildered and bewildering man.

I have met no American who has agreed with me on this. Indeed, almost nothing in the foregoing is likely to please American readers of Faulkner. Some do, I fear, belong to that class of avant-garde critics who "cannot afford" to be exasperated by writers of Faulkner's eminence. But most of his readers have no critical reputation to protect or establish. Leaving out of account those who read him for his "sexiness," so far as I have been able to understand, his appeal lies in his topical reflection of a widespread bewilderment, his nearness to his readers' own awareness of frustration and anger. They do not mind that he asserts nothing, that he not only reflects chaos but is chaotic himself. On the contrary, they enjoy the spectacle of the man struggling with his own chaos. It is like all-in wrestling. They do not mind that the world he has been creating in his imagination is a world after the Flood. They like such imaginings, provided they are dramatic enough. They are not in the least perturbed that he invokes a concept of tradition which is not the handing on of the wisdom of the generations but the denial of it. On the contrary, if one says, "But to Faulkner all tradition is impotent!" they will reply, "Perhaps it *is!*" They are not put off by his barbarous language. On the contrary, they are prepared to see in it a new Altamira. And they will, in passing, draw our attention to various plausible sources of his style: such as the political rhetoric of the South, the punch-drunk religious fervor of the Baptist backwoods preacher, the folk mentality of the South with its love for fantasy and exaggeration, the Negro tradition. And if one asks whether these influences are part of a fructive pattern which he would have been wiser to ignore, one may well be met by the sort of statement Mr. Malcolm Cowley makes about the Yoknapatawpha Saga: that "all his books in the saga are part of the same living pattern: it is this pattern *and not the printed volumes in which part of it is recorded* that is Faulkner's real achievement."

It must be evident that all such responses to Faulkner's

work are on the farthest periphery of literary criticism, if
not quite outside it. What has, indeed, constantly puzzled —
and entertained — me about such attitudes is that they are so
often maintained by disciples of an otherwise severely ra-
tional-analytical "higher criticism." They are, ultimately, ex-
pressions of hope and faith: that Faulkner is not only a very
fine writer, but an originator whose progeny will emerge in
the generations to come. They pre-empt criticism and make
all analysis irrelevant.

I nevertheless prefer to believe that there are explanations
for Faulkner's outlook and methods which are not beyond
understanding, and I have attempted to offer a few. One last
"explanation" I reserve to this point, since it happened to
come to me from an American — an old Southern aristocrat
lady who had sensibly enjoyed reading Faulkner for a very
sound and simple reason. "He writes very well," she said,
"for a man who writes about poor white trash." What she
meant by this was that Faulkner is not really in the oldest
Southern tradition at all, does not know it and does not understand it. The people he knows are, whether poor white
trash or not, people without intelligence or culture, people
with (like himself) comparatively shallow roots in the South,
not people made and marked by the full force of Southern
traditions. He is not, in other words, writing about a defeated South; he is writing about a wrecked and corrupted
South. The Snopes and their ilk are the only people he
really knows. The true race of Sartoris is outside his gamut;
what he produces as Sartorises are romanticizations. Not being informed by the finest traditions of the pre-Civil War
South, all he has to handle are the shards and broken scraps
of an old, lost, rich and complex life. He reflects most per-

suasively the ruin, the despair and the night. Nothing of so much that was fine and fructive and hopeful emerges. No wonder "tradition" to him is impotent.

One of the truest things said about him was said by Mr. Henry Nash Smith in that tiny periodical devoted to his work, called *Faulkner Studies:** "He seems often to be battling publicly with something deep and hostile within himself which he cannot see or define. It is this struggle which causes readers to turn again to books which repel and attract them almost indistinguishably." With which I put the shrewd remark of one of my American students: that I am unfit to speak about this man, because my approach to literature is too like that of French critics, through the intelligence, seeking an intelligence — and this man is without an intelligence.

I find that I can admire Faulkner better as a man than as a writer; except when he is being a humorous writer. He has felt inescapable urges through pity, and passion, towards ideals that he can vaguely feel but never express. His Nobel Prize speech, his commencement address at Pine Manor Junior College, in Wellesley, were eloquent of this in the nobility of their aspirations combined with the total unintelligibility of their ideas. It is his great spirit that pulls him through, and it is, I think, for his spirit that he is to be most admired. If one is insistent on asking for something more, one will always leave him deeply dissatisfied, as I always do.

As for the relation of Faulkner's work to the general theme of these essays, it must be unnecessary to underline it. He sees man only as martyr, a creature whose bravery can receive no sanction from a world of doom.

* Summer 1953, Vol. II, No. 2. "William Faulkner and Reality."

ERNEST HEMINGWAY

Men without memories

O NE of the most revealing things about the fiction of
Ernest Hemingway is that — with the exception of a
very few short pieces and his one really unsatisfactory novel,
To Have and Have Not — he has so far not written about his
life in the United States. In most fiction a writer's youth and
atavisms lie close to the surface of his thought. One can
nearly always trace back the grown man in his own work to
formative impressions and influences in his early life. They
may have been no more than a springboard, or something to
struggle with and cast off, or something to revert to as to an
obsession, but they are always known; he makes them
known. Only here and there does one get as much as a hint
from Hemingway's novels that he ever had parents, a childhood and a home. This self-bereavement is too unusual not
to be significant.

It is true that certain accidents in his life could have occasioned it; such as the fact that he learned his trade as a writer in Europe while stationed in Paris for a Toronto newspaper from 1921 onwards; or that he had his first adult home in Paris, as a husband and a father; or that practically all his literary friendships were formed in Paris; or even that he found plenty to write about in Europe, in his wartime experiences on the Italian front in 1918 when he was a slender youth of nineteen, or during the Spanish Civil War as a mature man, or in his many journeys through Europe and the Near East as a working journalist or sportsman. But such accidents have only a secondary or diminished power over an artist. The man who is not an artist will adapt his nature to chance; the artist adapts chance to his own nature. This may be less evident, or even less necessary, for an artist working in a tradition or school — though even there it is still to a greater or lesser degree necessary according to the originality of the artist — but it is absolutely necessary for the artist who is an individualist. And Hemingway explicitly insists on individuality in art, saying, "All art is done only by the individual. The individual is all you ever have and all schools only serve to classify their members as failures." He is not, in short, the sort of writer who would have willingly allowed his aesthetic to be molded so far as this by the fall of the dice, and his work clearly shows it. It could not, for instance, be a mere accident that none of his heroines is American — unless one counts Gordon's wife or Harry's wife in *To Have and Have Not* as heroines. His heroines are all Italian, English and Spanish, an exclusion of American womanhood that could be described as an un-American inactivity. (He was kind enough to Dorothy Bridges in *The Fifth Column* to say

that her name might have been Nostalgia. But Margot Macomber, and all that Wilson the hunter says about her,
makes up for that momentary lapse.) And while it is true
that all his central male figures are Americans, it is not unfair to say that, in so far as they are all aspects of himself,
they are all reflections of that primal extirpation. He must
have either cut away his youth deliberately, or been obliged
to do so by one of those seeming compulsions of nature
which are indistinguishable from the satisfaction of personal
desire. In either case, since every writer's aesthetic is formed
by the compulsions of his inmost being, this thing may bring
us very close to the core of his personal temperament, and
may ultimately throw light on his attitude to life.

One thing it does make clear. Like Faulkner he is subject
to a metaphysic of time which is his own creation. It is the
opposite of Faulkner's, for whom the human will is dominated by heredity, so that the present and future are, therefore, devoid of autonomy, and in practice nonexistent. (If
Faulkner burned incense to any old pagan philosopher he
should burn it to Heraclitus.) Hemingway, on the contrary,
came early to believe, or to make himself believe, that the
individual human will is autonomous and absolute. There is
nothing Jansenistic about Hemingway; if anything he is at
the opposite pole — a Pelagian. But he does believe that the
will is so constantly in jeopardy that it can assert itself only
briefly — in what I call a sort of captive now, which thereby
becomes a cardinal element in his technique and aesthetic.

We cannot tell exactly when he established his mind in
this tactical position. He himself encourages us to put it
around 1922, on his return from the Near East and the
searing experiences of the war between the Turks and the

Greeks, but he did not, so far as I know, articulate it until he began to write *Death in the Afternoon* around 1927. The cardinal passage has often been quoted:

I had just come from the Near East, where the Greeks broke the legs of their baggage and transport animals and drove and shoved them off the quay into the shallow water when they abandoned the City of Smyrna, and I remember saying (to Gertrude Stein) that I did not like the bullfights because of the poor horses.

I was trying to write then and I found the greatest difficulty, aside from knowing truly what you really felt, rather than what you were supposed to feel, and had been taught to feel, was to put down what really happened in action; what the actual things were which produced the emotions you experienced.

In writing for a newspaper you told what happened and, with one trick and another, you communicated the emotion aided by the element of timeliness which gives a certain emotion to any account of something that has happened on that day; but the real thing, the sequence of motion and fact which made the emotion and which would be as valid in a year or ten years or, with luck and if you stated it purely enough, always, was beyond me and I was working very hard to try to get it. The only place where you could see life and death, i.e., violent death now the wars were over, was in the bullring and I wanted very much to go to Spain where I could study it. I was trying to learn to write, commencing with the simplest things, and one of the simplest things of all and the most fundamental was violent death. It has none of the complications of death by disease, or so-called natural death, or the death of a friend or someone you have loved or have hated, but it is death nevertheless, one of the subjects that a man may write of. I have read many books in which, when the author tried to convey it, he only produced a blur, and I decided this was either because the author had never seen it clearly or, at the moment of it, he had physically or mentally shut his eyes, as one might do if he saw a child that he could not possibly reach for aid, about to be struck by a train. In such a case I suppose he would probably be justified in shutting his eyes as the mere fact of the child being about to be struck by the train was all that he could convey, the actual striking would be an anticlimax, so that the moment before striking might be as far as he could represent. But in the case of an execution by firing squad, or a hanging, this is not true, and if these very simple things were to be made permanent, as, say, Goya tried to make them in *Los Desastres de la Guerra,* it could not be done with any shutting of the eyes. I had seen certain things, certain simple things of this sort that I remember, but through taking part in them, or, in other cases, having to write of them immediately after and consequently noting the things I needed for instant recording, I had never been able to study them as a man might, for instance, study the death of his father or the hanging of someone, say, that he did not know and would not have to write of immediately after for the first edition of an afternoon newspaper.

So I went to Spain to see bullfights.

He saw about fifteen hundred of these "certain definite actions," close up to the eye of the camera, compressed in time and space.

He was interested, we note, in three things. The first was that, for the comparatively *concentrated spans of time* during which the fights lasted, he found that he could summon enough strength of mind to observe things calmly and clinically, somewhat like a medical student watching a surgical operation in the illuminated pit of a hospital amphitheater. The second was that he was able, over many repetitions of the same experience, to accumulate enough honesty to *purge his emotions* of all reactions inherited from prejudice or preconception. Here again, the essence of this discipline was that the total experience had to be submitted to conscious feeling in temporal isolation in order to be washed clean of all previous association. The moment was arrested, captured, taken out of context, and held in suspense. When this was done the pure fact, calmly observed, and the pure disinfected feeling amounted to "what really happened." The third thing that interested him at the bullfight was the essential drama being played out by the chief actors: *the fight between life and death.* We will return later to this third interest.

The first part of his problem and his solution of it are epitomized touchingly and amusingly by his reference to his unsatisfactory experiences as a journalist, and if we are searching for his first inklings that such a problem existed in literature, it may well take us behind 1922 to those days when he was a cub reporter on the ambulance run for the Kansas City *Star,* a youth in his teens, fiddling eagerly with his pencil in preparation for the "what really happens." He soon found himself, as he afterwards did in Europe, foiled by the pressure of the clock; forced to play for quick effects by exploiting a mechanical audience reaction, playing, that means, on those very things which in watching the bullfights later on he was to try so hard to eliminate in himself. For the essence of journalism is that nothing is ever really arrested or isolated in time. On the contrary, the journalist always subserves time to that perishable flux which we call the times. (How well named all those papers are which call themselves *Il Tempo, Le Temps, The Times.*) The journalist is in this sense literally a timeserver, conforming to that vast, ephemeral complex of fleeting conventions, prejudices, inhibitions, evasions and plain lies which every newspaper grandiosely calls its tradition, sometimes even more vaingloriously its policy, and from which no journalist is, or ever can be, free. Even if he is only writing about an automobile crash, his story becomes at once part and parcel of a general evanescence, here today, gone tomorrow. Only the artist can hope to cut himself off from recurrent mortality, and he does it simply by realizing that the corollary of time is eternity — the one subject never by any chance mentioned in newspapers. The most striking illustration of this is Proust, seeking always to capture the essence of the moment as if he were a magician able to preserve forever a drop of dew that falls on the palm of a childish hand.

Hemingway's aesthetic is based, to an exaggerated degree, on this technique of the captive now. He records experience with a stop watch. Click, and his story begins; click, and it is finished. No past; no future; no memory; no consequences, or at least none that promise any lasting effect.

With the exception of *Farewell to Arms,* the timetable is of the briefest, as if time were being snatched from death. *For Whom the Bell Tolls* occupies only sixty-eight hours. *The Sun Also Rises* occupies, for its main action, one week. *Across the River and Into the Trees* occupies a single week end. The old man fights his fight with the sea in about forty-eight hours. *To Have and Have Not* is all over in a couple of days. It is "as though something were hurrying us and we could not lose any time together," Catherine Barkley says. Jordan and Cantwell and Henry all have the same sense of there being no time to lose. What is pressing them all is the old enemy of the now, the tragic, timeless, eternal element

that brings the will into being, that will sooner or later destroy it but, if the will has in the meantime asserted itself,
cannot defeat it. So we get those six novels from *The Sun
Also Rises* to *The Old Man and the Sea*, cut off from the
past and leading to no future. Professor Carlos Baker has
well said that Hemingway's novels are screened at both
ends; pointing out also that with a few notable exceptions
all Hemingway's characters are, therefore, oddly rootless.
"They seem to come from nowhere, move into the now and
here, and depart again for nowhere after the elapsed time of
the novels." His characters fight out their battles on a lone
peak of time, like an Alpine peak cut across by a cloud, so
that those on the top of the mountain do not see and are indifferent to the temporate qualities of life in the valley, with
its trains and ships and roads and rivers and lakes leading
hither and thither, far and wide, according to timetables
that have as little to do with those remote Alpine dramas as
the Alps have to do with those who do not challenge them.

The illustration from style is equally notable. Compare
his curt periods with those wandering, parenthetic sentences
of Faulkner, long as the endless continuum which he calls
"time." As fact begins and ends for Hemingway with its first
appearance and its physical conclusion, so do his sentences.
So, one of the very first stories he published, "Up in Michigan," begins thus:

> Jim Gilmore came to Horton's Bay from Canada. He
> bought the blacksmith shop from old man Horton. Jim was
> short and dark with big mustaches and big hands. He was a
> good horseshoer and did not look much like a blacksmith
> even with his leather apron on. He lived upstairs above the
> blacksmith's shop and took his meals at A. J. Smith's.

As a rule, the sentences are about two lines in length, under twenty words. Now and again when he becomes garrulous we are involved in a sentence of as many as thirty-seven words.

This first book also contained ten poems, of which the first is a frank declaration of his stylistic method:

> *The mills of the gods grind slowly;*
>   *But this mill*
> *Chatters in mechanical staccato.*
>   *Ugly short infantry of the mind,*
> *Advancing over difficult terrain,*
>   *Make this Corona*
> *Their mitrailleuse.*

It was the style he forged, with the firm hammer blows of a village smith, to express his aspect of reality. It is evidently not a style that would have suited Henry James, or Proust, or Faulkner, or any man for whom each fact is wrapped in a cocoon of past associations, suggestions, implications, or traditions, and in expressing which the eye must lift from the object, and memory and thought begin to dilate and expand — and language with them.

We begin to see why Hemingway confiscated his own youth. We see that he was being entirely faithful to himself when he blandly made, also in *Death in the Afternoon,* the startling statement, one of the most startling statements ever made by a writer, that "memory, of course, is never true." * In

---

* He is speaking of criticism and the individual talent, which he considers the sole talent. "The individual is all you have and all schools only serve to classify their members as failures." The individual artist "goes beyond what has been done or known and makes something of his own." But there are long gaps between these original artists, and critics remember only the old ones, and see many false ones, and trust only to memory instead of feel-

that one sentence childhood, home, parents, relatives, inherited wisdom (or unwisdom), all traditions, all atavisms, the entire testament of the past are, if not dismissed, at least challenged boldly. And yet he was right — as for himself. There is an interesting illustration of this in his second book, *In Our Time:* the story called "An Indian Camp."

In this delicate little story, rich and tender with human feeling, Nick Adams's father, a physician like Hemingway's father, rows over to an Indian settlement to deliver a baby by Caesarian section, using only a jacknife and nine-foot tapered gut leaders. When it is all over and the mother's screams have subsided, the doctor takes a look at the husband, who has all the time been lying silent in the bunk above her, his face to the wall. He is dead. Unable to bear his wife's screams he has cut his throat with a razor. As doctor and son walk back to the boat they talk a bit about what has happened and this is how the story ends:

> "Is dying hard, Daddy?"
> "No, I think it's pretty easy, Nick. It all depends."
> They were seated in the boat, Nick in the stern, his father rowing. The sun was coming up over the hills. A bass jumped, making a circle in the water. Nick trailed his hand in the water. It felt warm in the sharp chill of the morning.
> In the early morning, sitting in the stern of the boat, with the father rowing, he felt quite sure that he would die.

The story, while it is tender and moving, and perfectly told, has one fatal weakness. It is not by Hemingway. It is derivative. In writing like that, he allowed into the story an

ing. He, thereupon, utters the sweeping statement "Memory, of course, is never true."

element — very slight, a mere flicker, no more than the breath of a May fly on a still lake — which is shockingly false to his temperament, and which never again appears in the whole run of his work: the element of self-pity. It is a legitimate and natural way of looking at the shortness of life, but it is not the way of a man for whom, at the time he was writing, the shortness of man's life, so far from being an invitation to pity, is a challenge to courage. It is not an attitude which can be related to his almost obsessional insistence on facing the fact of death in order to assert the autonomy of the will.

We begin to see that he has two possible meanings in mind in saying that "memory, of course, is never true." The first is that it is untrue not in a practical or moral sense but in the craftsman's sense; as when we say that a thing is off the true, or when we speak of a true balance. It is a professional warning, not at all unlike what a golf professional means when he tells us to keep our eye on the ball. Once lift your eye from the actuality of the moment, he seems to say, and you are distracted, deceived, deflected, lose focus, strike without accuracy, and the next thing you know you are in the rough of the sentimental, or the bogus. The implication, of course, is that after a long apprenticeship to the actuality of the moment you may stop being a catechumen and begin to apply what you have learned to a variety of experiences. But this is more than remembering, since each case is different from what you had learned. You apply the laboratory experiment under new conditions. It is what every professional does, whether he is a plumber or an orthodontist. This can be the only technical meaning to his use of the word *true*. Otherwise everything that Dickens,

Daudet, Turgenev, Chekov, Gide — the examples are endless — wrote about their childhood would be false.

The second meaning I put forward more tentatively, and
if it represents a part of the thought which impelled the
statement, it is much more interesting. It implies that, to
him, memory is much too coarse a sieve to hold the delicate
and fearful intrinsicality of the past. It may be thought
that this is much too tremulous and tender an attitude to
attribute to a writer of Hemingway's texture. It may be held
that there is nothing in the course of his work to justify us in
thinking him capable of such a respectful feeling for that
past which he has seemed to ignore or to dismiss with an
almost brutal rejection. Yet what I am suggesting in this
essay is that this very rejection arises from the fact that there
is in Hemingway's nature a tenderness which he normally
represses or conceals. The few occasions — as in "An Indian
Camp" — when he does release it are revealing precisely
because they are few.

We shall never know — or not unless fuller biographical
material, such as intimate letters or the recollections of
youthful contemporaries, reveals his secret — why he has
this inhibition about the past. Was his home life particularly
painful? Were there domestic scenes that hurt him? (We
know that his father subsequently committed suicide.) Has
all his son's subsequent life been a way of winning in art
what the father lost in life? As one might also say of
Joyce? Could it possibly be that he who has made so much
of heroism is afraid of tenderness? All we can do is to feel
our way behind those suppressions of which he himself has
given us a few hints; as in that superb and touching story
"Fathers and Sons" in the volume *Winner Take Nothing*.

Here Nick Adams does remember his home, his childhood and his father.

> Like all men with a faculty that surpasses human requirements, his father was very nervous. Then, too, he was sentimental, and, like most sentimental people, he was both cruel and abused. Also he had much bad luck, and it was not all of it his own. He had died in a trap that he had helped only a little to set, and they had all betrayed him in various ways before he died. All sentimental people are betrayed so many times.

Perhaps Hemingway's fear of the past is a form of anti-sentimentality? The pose Nick adopts — the only possible word here is *pose* — when speaking of his dead father's face is illuminating:

> On the other hand his father had the finest pair of eyes he had ever seen and Nick had loved him very much and for a long time. Now, knowing how it had all been, even remembering the earliest times before things had gone badly was not good remembering. If he wrote it he could get rid of it. He had gotten rid of many things by writing them. But it was still too early for that. There were still too many people. So he decided to think of something else. There was nothing to do about his father and he had thought it all through many times. The handsome job the undertaker had done on his father's face had not blurred in his mind and all the rest of it was quite clear, including the responsibilities. He had complimented the undertaker. The undertaker had been both proud and smugly pleased. But it was not the undertaker that had given him that last face. The undertaker had only made certain dashingly executed repairs of doubtful artistic merit . . .

The roughness does not ring true. What does ring true is the only half-suppressed feeling.

He makes the Colonel in *Across the River and Into the Trees* resist sentiment in a not dissimilar way when thinking of the one-eyed Arnaldo:

> He only loved people, he thought, who had fought or been mutilated. Other people were fine and you liked them and were good friends; but you only felt true tenderness and love for those who had been there and had received the castigation that everyone receives who goes there long enough. So I'm a sucker for crips, he thought, drinking the unwanted drink. And any son of a bitch who has been hit solidly, as every man will be if he stays, then I love him. Yes, his other, good, side said, you love them. I'd rather not love anyone, the Colonel thought. I'd rather have fun. And fun, his good side said to him, you have no fun when you do not love. All right. I love more than any son of the great bitch alive, the Colonel said, but not aloud.

There are other hints of buried feelings. There is the poem "Along with Youth," in which he remembers, sadly, old, lost things, a stuffed bird, piles of old magazines

> . . . *drawers of boyish letters*
> *And the line of love.*
> *They must have ended somewhere.*

Or the poem beginning "All of the Indians are dead" (reminding us of Nick Adams's first affair with an Ojibway girl): the long prairies, the moon rising, the ponies dragging at their pickets, ending movingly with:

Pull an arrow out:
If you break it
The wound closes.

(Meaning, I take it, that it is an Indian belief that if you break the arrow that wounded you the wound will close.)

. . . The wound closes.
Salt is good too
And wood ashes.
Pounding it throbs in the night —
(or is it the gonorrhea).

Another roughness which rings false; a dodging away from the brief honest confession that an old wound still "throbs in the night." Is this secret night his other private world that he has so rarely faced in print? The little, sad, derivative final verse in the book seems to say so:

For we have thought the longer thoughts
And gone the shorter way.
And we have danced to devils' tunes,
Shivering home to pray;
To serve one master in the night,
Another in the day.

His third and chief interest in the bullfight, we remember, was not the bulls, or the matadors, or the technique of the fight, or the crowds, or anything living. It was, he says so himself, violent death: that subject which he describes as "one of the simplest things of all and the most fundamental," and which, at the brief moment of the kill in the arena, gave him a sensation of immortality.

Let us look at two brief descriptions of that moment,

noting first that "immortality" seems to mean to Hemingway not, as it means to most of us, an extramortal eternity but a form of timelessness transported into mortal life. The clock is stopped. There is death and yet there is no death, change yet no dissolution. The moment held in suspense stops the world of nature. It is not an uncommon fancy with poets. "Helen, make me immortal with a kiss." Death cannot touch me, the patriot thinks proudly even while the ax is being sharpened beneath his window. We will also note that the conflict he describes between life and death, time and eternity, is not occurring in the ring at all. It is a conflict taking place within Hemingway's imagination. Naturally, it could only take place there, since time is itself a purely imaginative or intellectual concept which exists as an extramental reality only in its physical implications, of which the main one is change. We see change and we think time; as when we see the tobacco ash floating into the ash tray, leaves falling, our bodies withering. Actually, to halt time would be not only to halt change but to postpone death and therefore put an end to life. It is this imaginative experience that Hemingway is describing when he tells us about the sense of suspension he felt when watching the *faena:*

> The *faena* that takes a man out of himself and makes him feel immortal while it is proceeding, that gives him an ecstasy that while it is momentary is as profound as any religious ecstasy; moving all the people in the ring together and increasing in emotional intensity as it proceeds, carrying the bullfighter with it, he playing on the crowd through the bull and being moved as it responds in a growing ecstasy of ordered, formal, passionate, increasing disregard for death

that leaves you, when it is over, and the death adminis-
tered to the animal has made it possible, as empty, as
changed, and as sad as any major emotion will leave you.

And again:

> Now the essence of the greatest emotional appeal of bull-
> fighting is the feeling of immortality that the bullfighter
> feels in the middle of a *faena* and that he gives to the spec-
> tators. He is performing a work of art, and he is playing with
> death, bringing it closer, closer, closer to himself. . . . He
> gives the feeling of his immortality, and, as you watch it, it
> becomes yours.

Provided, that is, you also see it as a work of art, provided
you also see it imaginatively, and not just as a spectacle of a
straight fight between a plain man and a plain bull. But
Hemingway is asking us in all his work to see life imaginatively, and when he describes something in life — a fight, a
battle, a love scene, a fisherman playing his fish — it is not
really the *thing* which is important, to him or for us, but
whatever it is that those things symbolize for him, and for
us; or to put it in less pompous and suspect language, whatever it is that these things "mean" to him or "say" to him
about the nature of life in general and especially about man
living in this mortal world. The reason he chooses those
short moments and those elemental characters he employs,
people who never think, in any profound sense of that word
— when now and again they try to "think," like Jordan or
Colonel Cantwell, the effect is embarrassing — is (I suppose
at this date one may add "of course") that these general
meanings and sayings of life have clustered in his mind over

the years around a hard, clear, simple, nuclear admiration
for heroism in moments of crisis.

I hope it is now safe for me to write down plainly what I
have been leading up to all along: that it would be absurd to
develop a criticism of this man's work on naturalistic or
realistic lines. Certainly he uses the same shapes and forms
of nature, men and women, places and things, that everybody uses who speaks in terms of any art. Certainly it is true
that he presents those physical people and things with a
graphic, naturalistic power not often surpassed by any contemporary. It is also true that many people read him for this
graphic presentation alone, and are therefore sometimes
puzzled to see why he should be taken so seriously as an
artist. They have failed to see that although his shapes and
forms are ordinary men and women, his true subject,
which is death, and everything in life that conspires with it
to make men weak, and everything fine in man that fights
against it, lifts his men and women, *for their great moment,*
as far above the ordinary as, say, Ibsen in his own way up-
lifts such superficially ordinary characters as Hedda or Norah
or the Hilda of *The Master Builder.*

One can go further. Most novelists deal with character, or
characterization. Hemingway does not. He may think he
does, but that is irrelevant. What he deals with is personality.
Character is a public, social thing formed almost always by
society. Personality is a private, secret thing formed almost
always by the man and the woman alone. It is a distinction
which has been observed by many people who have written
about the individual and the soul. Yeats made it, saying that
personality is what remains when the dross of outward
things falls away in moments of great tragedy and personal-

ity burns with a pure adamantine flame. Catholic thinkers, like Garrigou Lagrange and Maritain, have insisted on the same distinction, pointing out that the modern worship of "individualism" is often completely false and deluded, since what is worshiped in the end is a mere digit, a cipher in a bureaucrat's blueprint, not a personal man; and that all that really matters is this unique personal thing which makes each soul incapable of being duplicated. This is why novelists who deal with character rather than personality seek always for the external indications and stress them. One is told what politics a man has, what tobacco he smokes, what dress he favors, what his ideas are, where he lives. The color of his hair, his ties, his idiosyncrasies are exploited. In the end one may see a man as one might know him in the club or on a ship. Writers who are interested in personality despise these trappings. They are thinking so hard about the noumenal flame in the man that they cannot be bothered with the external phenomena. If we examine Hemingway's stories we will find that he never bothers very much about externals of this order. What do we know, of this order, about, say, Nurse Barkley? Or Jordan? Or recall that fine story "The Undefeated," about the all-but-undefeated bull and the all-but-defeated matador? We cannot visualize the matador, tell anything about him except that he is at once half a coward and altogether a hero. Hemingway does not care about anything else pertaining to him. He is concerned only with the essences of people as they reveal themselves — and only as they reveal themselves — in certain testing moments, great and small.

He is not interested in anything that could be called reasonable, or that could be tested by what the world calls common sense. He is after another sort of common sense: that gallant form of common sense which is the acceptance of the facts of danger and death. Otherwise he might seem deliberately, and challengingly, to have chosen the sort of conflicts in which reason has no place. The whole action of *For Whom the Bell Tolls* centers on the blowing up of a bridge which is to be the hub of an attack that the hero knows will be a tragic fiasco. Pablo, in that novel, might strike anybody accustomed to fighting as the only sensible man in the whole crowd — and he is deliberately pictured as a broken man and a coward. But Hemingway might ask: Has heroism any sense to it beyond the fact that it is heroism just because it has no rational defense — that it is a form of mystical sacrifice? He knows that the behavior of the unhappy Francis Macomber is quite devoid of our sort of common sense. He forces us to see, in *The Old Man and the Sea*, that the whole point of the old man's fight with the fish is that his gallant struggle is pointless, rationally speaking, since he will return at the end of it all with nothing but a skinned skeleton.

To this we must reply that Hemingway either cheats or is blithely inconsistent. We may recall, for example, the Fascist captain who is killed by Sordo's stratagem on the hilltop. Hemingway, as if he were remembering the fun Bluntschli makes of the heroic ass in *Arms and the Man*, presents this captain to us not as a hero but as a foolhardy fanatic.

This is where his *mystique* of heroism becomes ankle-deep. For we suddenly realize that heroism for heroism's sake is not quite good enough, and we begin, uneasily, to probe into the nature of heroism itself. We ask: Is a gangster not also a brave man? In other words, we come to the point where we feel that it is impossible for any writer to deal satisfyingly with heroism without considering values, which means the weighing up of motives, which means the development of an implicit criticism of the forces that produce these motives, which means in the long run that the author has to imply his own norm. Put oneself in the place of that Fascist captain on Sordo's hilltop. He made a personal decision. Why? Pride, vanity, ignorance, loyalty to a political system, hate, weakness disguised as strength, a spirit of self-sacrifice for an ideal? The possible reasons are endless. Hemingway blandly calls his state of mind "exaltation" and denies him the palm he gives to Sordo, chiefly, if not entirely, because he was a bad tactician. It is unsatisfying.

The evident truth, as most of us see it, about heroic deeds is that they are done, as a rule, for two main reasons: in the name of a system, or an ideal, or a religion, or some other social nexus which the hero chooses to represent; or else for some wholly personal vision. But whether the motivation be public or private we cannot dissociate the action from the impulse. Otherwise the gangster, the murderer, the pimp, the kidnaper dying bravely would be entitled to call himself a hero. Mrs. Cecil Woodham Smith's recent history of the famous Charge of the Light Brigade — which those of us who are in our fifties or sixties will remember chiefly from Tennyson's glorification of the "gallant six hundred" — has led many of us to think that Lord Cardigan was simply Bluntschli's heroic ass all over again. If we think otherwise we will do so only by relating the incident to a large network of ideas connected with such matters as military discipline, *esprit de corps*, the way empires are finely built and

finely defended — in short, with all those things that come
under the head of the word *tradition,* and which are entirely rejected or neglected or unconsidered by Hemingway.

A good illustration of the weaknesses and pitfalls of a
mystique divorced from tradition is *Across the River and
Into the Trees.* Here, for once, Hemingway most unwisely
put himself — through his two main characters, the Colonel
and the *Contessina* — into contact with the past. He stepped
into one of the oldest, most complicated and most traditional milieus in the world — the Venetian aristocracy — all
the more complicated because in our time it is in its probably final stage of disintegration. He seems instinctively to
have seen the dangers, since he does not set his story among
the villas of the Brenta, does not even touch any of the last
few remaining private *palazzi,* but sets it, chiefly, in one of
the big modern hotels; thereby refusing to admit that it
could possibly have been necessary for Colonel Cantwell to
have approached cautiously or deviously, explored patiently
the complex procedures of the world he has invaded. We
never discover, for example, how this American officer managed to become intimate with a *contessina,* though it could,
no doubt, have happened quite easily, by luck or design —
on the Lido, in Harry's Bar, at a diplomatic cocktail party.
The reason is plain. If we were to be told how it happened
Hemingway would have become involved in explanations of
the social and moral conventions of Venice. He would
thereby have had to start to think, weigh values, become
aware of nuances in the relationship he describes. His colonel would have had to become a character totally different
to the thoughtless, typical Hemingway type that he is.

What the Colonel does is what Lord Cardigan did, and if the young lady had been a real person and not a Rugby player's pipe dream she would have felt at the end of it all like a flower bed after a Newfoundland had crashed through it. That she apparently takes it all for granted means that whatever she was she was not a Venetian *contessina,* or else she was a rather special sort of Venetian *contessina,* and this has not been explained to us by the author.

By contrast how much better *The Sun Also Rises* is — I count it as far and away his best novel to date — precisely because here values do arise in the clash between the Left Bank expatriates' modes of life and the traditions represented by the bullfighter Romero. The theme is not overstated. It is no more than suggested in the opposition between the vitality and decency and dignity of an old race and the moral disintegration of the new intruders, so that the novel fumes in the memory like a thought that one can sense but not define. The fact that the *mystique* is capable of carrying such suggestions, but rarely does, can only mean that Hemingway is generally content to exploit it in a rather too simple way. The fact is that he probably knows the limits of his powers, and knows also what he likes to do, which is to use strong, bold colors, like a *Fauve* painter. But to have attempted to handle the Venetian story in this fashion was a grave misjudgment on his part.

There is something very American about all this. Americans like to talk about their Puritan origins, or their English forbears, or pay lip service to the influence of the various Christian churches, but their true avatars were the Red Indians. Somebody called Maupassant a *Huron de génie.* The term fits Hemingway perfectly, and it could be applied

equally well to a number of American writers of the so-
called tough school — except when they are dealing with
women, whose scent at once unmans them. The characters
of these writers are all out on a limb of life. They are lone
scouts. Hemingway never chose a less apt epigraph than
when he attached to *For Whom the Bell Tolls* Donne's "No
man is an island, entire of itself . . ." All his men are islands, and he does not, cannot and should not try to write
of men who are "a part of the maine."

No book showed this better than *For Whom the Bell
Tolls* itself. For here he was writing not about a man but
about a people, indeed, as time was to show, about a whole
world preparing for total war. It was a subject which de-
manded a consideration of all the traditional pieties that he
has deliberately excluded from his work, those ancient, often
inexpressible things that give sanctity and dignity to common life. If one compares this novel with that fine Spanish
trilogy of Arturo Barea, *The Forge, The Clash* and *The
Track*, one sees at once that what gives Barea's work so
much depth and force is the implicit sense of the multitude
of things that were at stake for Spain in the Civil War —
friendship and faith, boyhood memories, atavisms old as
time. I do not deny for a moment that it could have been
possible to have made an American the central figure of a
novel involving all those things if Hemingway had, say,
enough sense of humor or enough intimate knowledge of
Spanish life to intimate certain inevitable incongruities in
Jordan's behavior. The whole of that sleeping-bag incident,
for example, would, so treated, have become not embarrassing but revealing. As it was, Spanish readers of the novel
were dumfounded by the incident, realizing that a girl like

Maria could not conceivably have yielded so swiftly, above all within that tight society of the cave, to a total stranger. (It was Barea who pointed out that Hemingway was apparently confusing the mores of two regions in Spain, transferring the morality of a bullfighter's moll to a region where a very different set of conventions applies.) So, the novel is magnificent when dealing with scenes of action, in all of which Pilar and Pablo and El Sordo and the guerrillas steal the stage from Jordan, and unsatisfying when Jordan is being made to carry the theme of the national struggle. The result of making him a central figure is that in the end the arc of the story's movement is broken abruptly by his death, wherein he dwindles to a mere speck thrown off the whirling wheel of the Spanish tragedy. We follow the broken arc with unsatisfied eyes, eager to know what happened to the really important people, Pilar, Pablo, Maria and the others. The captive-now device was sadly inapplicable here, the effort to express in the usual brief space of time, in one corner of the arena, through a man who came from nowhere, had no past, is given no build-up, a theme far larger than so sketchy a character could possibly contain.

I think it is interesting to add, for it is highly revealing of the Americanism of all this, that when I said these things in public lectures in the United States I found that I provoked intense disagreement. My listeners said, in effect, sometimes rather angrily, "Jordan died finely! Is that not enough? What more do you want?" The discussion always took the same course from that point. *Me:* "But a gangster can die finely. Is that not enough?" *They:* "But Jordan was fighting Fascism!" *Me:* "Then why did Soviet critics of the novel say that if Hemingway had been a Communist it would have been a great book?" *They:* "What did the Communists mean by that? Did they want pro-Communist propaganda?" *Me:* "Possibly! Indeed probably! But what they thought they wanted was to know what precisely Jordan's ideas and values were, what made him anti-Fascist, what he hoped to achieve and what he hoped to leave behind." To this the answers were either that Jordan was fighting for democracy, or that he was fighting for his own soul, or that he left behind him a good example of courage, or that he rehabilitated Maria; but in the main the arguments concentrated on Jordan's personal integrity — and on democracy. I usually skipped democracy as being a pathless bog, and tried to narrow the argument to Jordan's personal vision of life. And there we always came to a dead end, for two reasons: the first being that to most of my listeners it apparently *is* enough to die bravely for some generally accepted but unexamined system; and the second and most important reason being that Hemingway has not told us enough about Jordan's mind. The captive-now device, the stop-watch click, had brought him on the stage with no more than a few scraps or tags from his past, just as it showed him off the stage without intimating what effect, if any, he had had on the lives of those with whom he had so briefly crossed paths.

The Hemingway *mystique* has sometimes been called, in a superficial, conversational way, a form of Stoicism. The comparison only serves to expose his shallowness. Indeed, it is to do grave injustice to Hemingway to evoke the complexity and variety of that noble philosophy, with its simultaneous belief in a wise and well-ordaining divinity and its frank acceptance of the facts of pain and practical evil; its con-

current belief in the power of the mind to control and enjoy
the urges of the body, to partake in the Epicureans' "beautiful arrangement of things," and to "pass from Nature to
Nature's God"; its effective blending of a life of useful
activity in service to others with a quasi-Oriental love of contemplation. To invite thoughts of that full and complex
mystique is only to be obliged to think what an unvarious
wash of color even the best of Hemingway's work has drawn
across the landscape of life. We must not invite such com-
parisons. Hemingway is not a thoughtful man. He has no
evident interest in social, moral or philosophical ideas at all.
He is not and never pretended to be an intellectual. He is a
man who loves gallant men and gallant animals. He is also a
man, and it is this which gives him his real stature also as
an artist who loves the gallant spirit, and he has roved the
world in search of that flame of the spirit in men and beasts.
To capture that flame, to record the moments in which it
burns most brightly, has been his life's design. But to explain
to us the origins of such moments, to give us their pedigree,
is beyond his power. So, as to the psychological reasons why
Francis Macomber did not grow up to be a Jordan, or why
Jordan did not grow up to be a Francis Macomber, he has
not even the inkling of an idea. How could he, having so
early decided to confiscate that element of past time during
which men are made whatever they finally are at the testing
hour?

It might seem that, having said that Hemingway has
wisely and shrewdly chosen his ground and his gamut in
accordance with his instinct for what he can do and cannot
do, I am now complaining that he has not done something
quite different. On the contrary, while properly pointing out

the limitations of his gamut I am trying to draw attention to the excellence of what he actually has achieved by insisting again that what he has achieved has nothing whatever to do with the naturalism with which he is usually associated, for which he is widely read, and which is the source of his widespread popularity. Properly assessed, this man is not a popular writer at all, any more than Graham Greene is a popular writer. To explain what I mean, let me quote Thierry Maulnier on the nature of all popular art:

> A great art never becomes popular unless it contains ideas and fatalities on the level of average experience, brings them into play on the epic level of violent or social conflict, illustrates them by imagery of an elementary nature. The reader responds to a work of art only in proportion as he finds in it whatever idea he has already formed of himself, of his own life. For the average man leads a double life. On the one hand, he is preoccupied by all the minor details of his daily existence; on the other hand, he is pleased by whatever provides him with an escape from his daily round, such as the sight of splendid self-sacrifice, finely wrought feelings, great causes of common interest — military, moral, humanitarian and so forth. To please the average man, art must always represent average destinies, which need not exclude grandeur or good style. There can, then, be no such thing as a popular art which is not either realistic, or epical, or moral.

He goes on, therefore, to say that, by contrast with all this, a Racine could never have been popular, because he rejected all local color and all those accidental trappings of time and place which always appeal to the romantic sentiment; not to speak of his subtlety, his hatred of sentimentality and tinsel sublimity, his aristocratic insistence on ignoring the representative, social citizen and on writing only about individ-

uals — in short, his exclusive interest in *l'essence de l'homme
et son tragique immuable.*

At first glance both Hemingway and Greene seem to be
well described by Maulnier's opening sentences. But are the
destinies which they describe "on the level of average experience"? Do we find images of ourselves in the Jordan of *For
Whom the Bell Tolls,* or in the whiskey priest of *The Power
and the Glory?* Perhaps if one were young enough, and romantic enough, one might wish to live vicariously with
Jordan, but I have to confess that as for myself — and I think
the same must be true for anyone over twenty-five — I could
no more identify myself with Jordan than I could identify
myself with the Cid, however deeply I may sympathize with
the idea of Jordan or the idea of the Cid. Jordan certainly
identifies himself with a great cause of common interest. But
does Lieutenant Henry in *A Farewell to Arms,* or anybody
in *The Sun Also Rises,* or the old man fighting the fish, or
Colonel Cantwell, or the smuggler in *To Have and Have
Not,* or any single character in the whole run of the short
stories?

The things in Hemingway that really please the populace
are the "local color and the accidental trappings of time and
place which always appeal to the romantic sentiment." Yet,
even here I think the populace is being, in the best possible
sense, given a complete illusion. Just as Hemingway's sup-
posedly "natural" conversations are completely artificial
(again in the best sense of the word), that is, stylized, non-
representational — compare them with a dictaphone recording of any actual conversation to see the difference between
reality and art — so, the deluded reader may find on looking
into the matter, are the doses of "local color and accidental

trappings." I leave him to test the matter for himself in as thorough a manner as he pleases, but I will here give a few brief examples to illustrate how Hemingway actually treats "local color."

The Sun Also Rises. Total description of the town of Bayonne:

> "Bayonne is a nice town. It is like a very clean Spanish town and it is on a big river. Already, so early in the morning, it was very hot on the bridge across the river.

Total description of the cathedral of Bayonne:

> We went out into the street again and took a look at the cathedral. Cohn made some remark about it being a very good example of something or other, I forget what. It seemed like a nice cathedral, nice and dim, like Spanish churches.

Total description of the Landes country:

> There were wide fire-gaps cut through the pines, and you could look up them like avenues and see wooded hills way off. About seven-thirty we had dinner and watched the country through the open window in the diner. It was all sandy pine country full of heather. There were little clearings with houses in them, and once in a while we passed a saw-mill. It got dark and we could feel the country hot and sandy and dark, and about nine o'clock we got into Bayonne.

A Farewell to Arms. Description of the country between Gorizia and Udine:

> . . . I looked at the country. The mulberry trees were bare and the fields were brown. There were wet dead leaves

on the road from the rows of bare trees and men were working on the road, tamping stone in the ruts from piles of
crushed stone along the side of the road between the trees.
We saw the town with a mist over it that cut off the mountains. We crossed the river and I saw that it was running
high. It had been raining in the mountains.

These are not "accidental trappings of time and place."
They are things that are always true, everywhere. They are
generally true, not true in a particular time and place. Always Hemingway seeks for these universal things. Earlier I
quoted the end of the story "An Indian Camp," with its
description of the morning on the lake. "The sun was coming
up over the hills. A bass jumped, making a circle in the
water. Nick trailed his hand in the water. It felt warm in the
sharp chill of the morning." That circle made by the bass
jumping is the mark of Hemingway's art. He gives us the
impression that we are there, at that moment, in that particular place, and yet that it is also a sliver of universal and
eternal truth. This is what I meant by saying that, properly
assessed, he is not a "popular" writer. He is, within his
honestly stated limits, and despite the weaknesses and idiosyncrasies that belong to the coarser element of his mind, a
writer whose subject is *l'essence de l'homme et son tragique
immuable*. I dare to say that Racine would have been
shocked by his stories, but that if he were patient enough
he would have come to understand and admire what Hemingway is seeking. Zola would not have been in the least
shocked by him, and would never have been able to understand what he is seeking. I place Hemingway, in his own
modest way, in the great and now almost defunct classical
tradition.

By his denial of the past and his concentration on the present (the captive now), Hemingway has succeeded in rediscovering in men a greater dignity than, I suspect, he had ever hoped to find in them. This is his achievement, and how few, how very few, modern writers have arrived so far! Had he not made this discovery he would have been confined to those graphic short stories and sketches which were his first stunned reactions to his experience of life. He persisted and he discovered. When any man does something like this he has won a great primal victory within his personality over all the enemies of promise: he has found a way out towards writing; he has conquered the blank page. After that the rest is a matter of a growing skill in the writing, and of an ever-developing personality.

I am not sure that Hemingway's personality has gone on developing. If it is to develop further he will now have to face up to the limitations of his central device, get more room to spread, humanize his *mystique* by considering — I choose that word — a greater variety of human problems. To do this he will have to summon up the energies of his soul for the greatest act of courage in his long and gallant struggle — the courage to face that past which he has so far buried away in the cupboard with the old dance programs, piles of letters and faded photographs, memories hitherto too painful to handle. If he can do this without injury to his great technical gifts as an apparently naturalistic writer his popularity will not suffer. The trouble will be that he may well have to sacrifice something of his pseudorealism that the populace so loves, and his colonels instead of calling abruptly for another Martini at the sight of anything in the nature of an intellectual problem — the Martini is Heming-

way's magical trap door — may have to pause and endure
the less easy and more troublesome experience of considering
more carefully whatever matter may be on hand. His work
could thereby (or in some other way which it is his task to
invent) become finer, and stronger, and take on much more
depth. His popular appeal would be almost certain to decline at once — unless his critics fight for him in a full
understanding of his problem as a writer, and as a man.

His place in this series of essays on the writer and the
Hero is evident: he is the only modern writer of real distinction for whom the Hero does in some form still live. The
price he pays for this is that his Hero is always as near as
makes no matter to being brainless, has no past, no traditions
and no memories. The traditional Hero who was the personi-
fication of some widely accepted norm occurs in Hemingway's work only in terms of the traditions of the Spanish
bullfight, or, as Arturo Barea pointed out apropos of *For
Whom the Bell Tolls*, he is borrowed and transferred from
those traditions. We may regret this exclusive glorification of
brute courage, strength, skill and grace, but I doubt if it is a
literary criticism to do so. It sounds much more like the sort
of social criticism to which Russian writers might be expected to be submitted in the literary columns of *Pravda*.
Yet, if we compare his hirsute heroes, who are outside tradition, with the thoughtful, sensitive, considering, gallant hero
of Evelyn Waugh's last two-volume novel, the entirely traditional and wholly anemic Guy Crouchback, the moral will
uncomfortably appear. A man can in our time be brave and
add a cubit of heroism to his height when fighting for himself; if he is fighting for a cause or an idea he can still be

brave, but instead of becoming a hero he may end up as a war criminal. The moral of Hemingway is that the only possible Hero of our times is the lone wolf. It is an idea wholly in accord with the spirit of the twenties, which he so well represents.

ELIZABETH BOWEN

Romance does not pay

WE may doubt reasonably that the novels of Miss Elizabeth Bowen would appeal very much to either William Faulkner or Ernest Hemingway. She has too much
awareness of tradition. One may believe that they do give
pleasure to Evelyn Waugh, if only for their subacid humor,
and their civilized atmosphere, and because one hears from
behind her civil façade that kind of *farouche* note which one
associates with teen-age delinquents about to break prison —
that is, leave home. More surprisingly at first glance one
knows from reviews and passing references that her work
has a certain appeal for Graham Greene. Yet, perhaps he
alone could explain to Faulkner and Hemingway that all
five have at least one thing in common. None of them is at
the center of gravity of contemporary society.

Elizabeth Bowen is detached by birth from that society

she describes. She is an Irishwoman, at least one sea apart from English traditions. She descends from that sturdy and creative subrace we call the Anglo-Irish. At least a part of her literary loyalties are with that long and honorable pedigree that goes back through Shaw, Joyce, George Moore, Somerville and Ross, Yeats, Wilde, Goldsmith, Sheridan, Burke, Swift and Berkeley to the forced marriage of two races, two islands. Born in 1900, she spent her childhood in County Cork and Dublin. She has written about her Dublin childhood in that delicate piece of autobiography *Three Winters*. She has written about her ancestral Cork home, a bare, tall, impressive, Italianate, limestone house under those North Cork hills where Spenser lived in exile, in her history of her home, *Bowenscourt*. She now lives there. In her novel *The Last September*, she has recorded with an effective blend of nostalgia and pain life in that part of Ireland and, I think, in that house during the troubled revolutionary period of the twenties. Her latest novel, *A World of Love*, also deals with provincial Irish life. Some of her short stories are set in Ireland. She has also written the history of a famous Dublin hotel, *The Shelbourne*. The rest of her books are set in London, the provinces or on the Continent, though there are also Irish sequences in *The House in Paris* and in *The Heat of the Day*. These Irish scenes show her at the peak of her form: she responds strongly to the native scene. She has come to know English life as an exile with an Irish home, a semialien, though entirely grateful and happy, observer.

The effects of this detachment seem to be mainly two. Malice would naturally be more free, and the play of sentiment more indulgent. It is a nice ambivalence. No English

writer can have quite the same liberty. One recalls Henry
James's remark in comparing the assertiveness of the French
mind with the diffidence of the English that whereas the
French always have the courage of their perceptions the
English have only the courage of their opinions ("when it
befalls that we have opinions"). He meant that it is in the
nature of the English tradition to nourish the precious fruits
of a national preference for the pragmatic view of life —
established social pieties, decorum, respect for others, a love
of fair play and good humor and decent reticence; all those
normal expansive tendencies which mitigate or abrade personal assertiveness and calm down nervous exasperation with
the way things happen to be. One has to be very cross, like
Evelyn Waugh, or very intense in a rather un-English way,
like Graham Greene, to let fly. A resident alien like Miss
Bowen may also stick in the barb. Shaw reveled in the role
of the Irish matador. But it also works the other way round
with the imported Janus *bifrons* from Ireland or the United
States or the Colonies. Katherine Mansfield, for example,
loved England even while she was exasperated by it, as her
Letters show. Janus may write about the new scene with even
more indulgence than a native; or write about the old scene
with more indulgence than if he had remained there.

Miss Bowen is indebted to another influence besides her
race and her exile to stiffen her own natural, shrewd intelligence, her own natural integrity as an observer. This is the
early influence of Flaubert. And when we recall the ro-
mantic-realist conflict within Flaubert we may see another
reason for thinking of Elizabeth Bowen as a bifrontal
writer. The conflict in her work is, in fact, not dissimilar.
She wavers between two methods of approach.

The essence of her way of seeing life is that, like the singer who was supposed to be able to break a champagne glass by singing at it, she exposes the brittleness of romance by soliciting it ruthlessly. Time, for her characters, is very far removed from Faulkner's continuum or Hemingway's feeling for events enclosed at both ends. It is a brittle moment, snatched from fate. Happiness in her novels is wrapped away, shoplifted, and always dearly paid for. God is the shopwalker who makes her characters pay, and we vulgar citizens, the run-of-the-mill of ordinary people, decent fathers of families, impatient of all youthful aberrations, cannot deny His justice.

Happiness may even have to be snatched between the moments. She pursues these golden if elusive hours on behalf of her heroines. So, in *The Last September* Francie Montmorency found that during her honeymoon, time had been "loose-textured, had had a shining undertone, happiness glittered between the moments." In *To the North* when Cecilia returns to her flat and looks about her at the unfamiliar familiar, "life here, still not quite her own, kept for those few moments unknown tranquillity." Happiness is thus interleaved in the book of life. It is a bonus, a wad of dollars smuggled through the customs of life. But to go after this happiness too hard is, one is led to feel, to wrench from life something that it can give only arbitrarily, like a fairy godmother. One is not therefore surprised to discover that there is nothing of the Hemingwayan will in her characters. They may seem willful; they are, in practice, the passive recipients of fate. All they receive from fate is passion, and this receipt is like a soldier's calling-to-the-colors. Her characters are conscripted by passion into action. Once in action they fight well, but what Arnold said of the Celt may be said of them: they go into battle and they always fall. It is true that they may also and for long have desired passion, but the desire is never so powerful as the impulse of chance. Her characters are all played upon.

There is a short story in her second book, *Ann Lee's,* written before she had published her first novel, which neatly illustrates this fateful element in all her later work. It is called "The Parrot." A young girl, Eleanor Fitch, is a companion to an old lady, Mrs. Willesden, in whose life nothing ever happens. One morning Eleanor accidentally lets her old lady's parrot fly away. She pursues the gaudy bird in its wayward flight from garden to garden until it pauses in the garden of a Mr. Lennicott, a novelist of doubtful repute, according to Mrs. Willesden. Palpitating, Eleanor enters the garden of this fabulous person, enters his house, meets him in his dressing gown, has the great adventure of capturing the multicolored bird with his assistance. When Lennicott kindly wishes to detain her, offering her fruit, she refuses. "Nobody had ever reached out for her like that so eagerly; she did not want to go back to that house of shut-out sunshine and great furniture where the parrot was royally carried from room to room on trays, and where she was nothing." Eleanor goes back unscathed to her dull routine, thinking "how world overlapped with world; visible each from the other, yet never to be one."

Now, I have a profound suspicion of that technique of criticism which elucidates the interior meaning of stories, and the secret meanings of an author's mind, by his unconscious use of symbols, but whether this brilliant and far-faring bird luring a potential Proserpine from garden to

garden to the haunts of Pluto is or is not — and I think it is
— in the full tradition of Flaubertian symbolism (the blue-
ness of Emma Bovary's dream curtains suggesting the Virgin,
and suchlike symbols) one may fairly use this fable as a symbol of one of Miss Bowen's favored types: the dreaming but
recusant girl. Longing but vigilant, troubled by her own
eagerness, she will, one fine day, follow the bright bird of
her dreams into the woods of life and suffer the fate of
Proserpine, or worse. There is an atmosphere of ancient
fable behind all of Miss Bowen's fiction. Her persons are
recognizable temperaments rather than composed characters. Flaubert merely overlays the fabulous. Her characters
are the modern, sophisticated, naturalistic novelist's versions
of primitive urges. One feels that if she had lived three
hundred and fifty years ago when passions rode freely and
fiercely she would have described the dreams that drove
Ophelia, Juliet and Desdemona to love and to death.

She conveys in a variety of ways this idea that it was all
arranged long ago, this idea of fate playing upon her people.
For one thing, her style matches her idea. Here is the opening page from *The Last September*. We note how the words
and phrases used suggested that everything here is subject
to some other agency:

> About six o'clock the sound of a motor, collected out of the
> wide country and narrowed under the trees of the avenue,
> brought the household out in excitement on to the steps. Up
> among the beeches a thin iron gate twanged; the car slid
> from a net of shadow down the slope to the house. Behind
> the flashing wind-screen Mr. and Mrs. Montmorency pro-
> duced — arms waving and a wild escape to the wind of her
> motor-veil — an agitation of greeting. They were long-prom-

ised visitors. They exclaimed, Sir Richard and Lady Naylor
exclaimed and signalled: no one spoke yet. It was a moment of happiness, of perfection.

The moment is perfectly fashioned, carefully observed, the
thin twang of the gate, the sun on the windscreen, the pe-
riod-fixing veil; but we note that we get, are meant to get,
throughout, the sensation of being exterior spectators, un-
fused with the characters, not vicariously doing anything.
And how little is actively done! The car does not make noise:
its noise is "collected . . . narrowed." The arriving guests
do not greet the people on the steps: they have "produced
an agitation of greeting." Mrs. Montmorency does not wave
her veil: it escapes. The hosts do not come out on the
steps: they are "brought out." The car does not drive down
to the house: it slides down, as if out of gear. We get an odd
sensation that something is missing, as if the sound track of
a film had gone dead. ("No one spoke yet.") What is missing is the active will, and this has been deliberately cut
off, or as deliberately as any author dominated by her personal way of seeing life can do anything deliberately.

The second paragraph of this opening page makes it clear
that the sense of outer forces at work has been conveyed as an
essential part of the theme. The heroine, Lois, appears on the
steps. We have already met this girl in "The Parrot." She is
one of Miss Bowen's most rewarding types: the girl emerg-
ing, awkwardly for herself and for others, into womanhood,
dreaming of romance, seeing herself in a role, troubled by a
sort of passionate virginity, equally thirsty for "life" and
inadequately wary of its complexities.

She knew how fresh she must look, like other young girls,
and clasping her elbows tightly behind her back tried hard

to conceal her embarrassment. The dogs came pattering out from the hall and stood beside her; above, the vast façade of the house stared coldly over the mounting lawns. She wished she could freeze the moment and keep it always. But as the car approached, as it stopped, she stooped down and patted the dogs.

Again, how excellently suggestive! She wished she could freeze the moment, but she suddenly rejects it; and as she does so, stooping down, overcome by reserve, the vast cold façade of the house, staring over the lawn, suggests the impersonal power of a presiding deity. The house, as soon begins to appear, is a clear symbol. It is a predominant agent affecting all those people, but pre-eminently Lois. It represents tradition, an enclosed world, her setting, in a sense her antagonist, her sacrificial altar. It is one of the many Big Houses, as we call them in Ireland, that have traditionally represented to the "mere Irish" an alien garrison. English soldiers, men of the so-called, and self-called, army of occupation, will come here to play tennis. Lois has already danced on the avenue with a young subaltern, Gerald Lesworth. He will be shot by the Sinn Feiners. The house will go up in flames on the last page of its last September. Houses, outside and inside, are almost an obsession — for which we are truly grateful — to this writer. She does not often see them comfortably; she describes them effectively, even if more often than not she makes them *unheimlich*, overpowering. Here are two examples of the effect of impassive power that she extracts from her domestic interiors: Lois goes upstairs to join her cousin, Laurence, a young Oxford intellectual, her male counterpart, typical of many of Miss Bowen's men in that he is clever but ineffectual. He is reading

in the anteroom because, characteristically, he is too lazy to
climb a floor higher to his own room; he has, also characteristically, brought the wrong book with him; and he sits, characteristically, in "one of a circle of not very comfortable shell-
back chairs that no one took seriously." Lois, also characteristically, often sits there chatting with him, her knee on
a chair because "it is not worth while to sit down." (Symbolists may make what they like of these marks of ineffectual-
ity in an *anteroom* through which other people are constantly passing about their business.) We read:

> The high windows were curtainless; tasselled fringes
> frayed the light at the top. The white sills, the shutters
> folded back in their frames were blistered, as though the
> house had spent a day in the tropics. Exhausted by the
> sunshine, the backs of the crimson chairs were a thin light
> orange; a smell of camphor and animals drawn from skins
> on the floor by the glare of the morning still hung like dust
> on the evening chill. Going through to her room at night
> Lois often tripped with her toe in the jaws of the tiger; a
> false step at any time sent some great claw skidding across
> the polish. Pale regimental groups, reunions a generation
> ago of the family or the neighbourhood gave out from the
> walls a vague depression. There were two locked bookcases
> of which the keys had been lost, and a troop of ebony ele-
> phants brought back from India by some one she did not
> remember paraded along the tops of the bookcases.

We become aware of dissolution, dissociation, a smother
of dusty days no longer remembered, things faded and exhausted and threatened by the jaw of the moth. The traveler
is forgotten, the keys are lost, the books unread, only the sun
has force, and that to wither. It is in this ambience that the
two young people converse, their lives before them in an ex-

hausted house. A still more striking and explicit example
occurs a little later when the guests and hosts are at dinner.
"The distant ceiling imposed on consciousness its blank
white oblong and a pellucid silence distilled from a hundred and fifty years of conversation waited beneath the ceiling." Can we feel anything but that the volition of these
people is dwarfed by the emanations of the house? And may
we not be fairly reminded of some Flaubertian interiors?
A sapless place, we must certainly think, for any young
girl. One could gather many such examples.

A third source of this sense of inertia is the grammar of the
style: the use of the passive voice, the impersonal pronoun,
the impersonal verb. "With him she felt committed by
speech itself to a display of such unfathomable silliness that
she might just as well come out with assertions surprising to
herself." Felt committed, and so talks like an automaton.
She had "a sense of return, of having been awaited." By
what? By whom? Lady Naylor breaks off a pleasant chat because "there was life to go on with, the duty of love and
pleasure fully discharged." Life is not actively enjoyed, it is
to be "got on with"; and love and pleasure are something besides life. It is as if invisible angels in helicopters are directing the emotional traffic when Mrs. Montmorency's mind
"lay back in silence, but there was a kind of sentinel in her
waiting for Hugo." Note how her past life with Hugo is
described — as she sees it:

> Their life through which they went forward *uncertainly*
> without the *compulsion* of tragedy was *a net* of small com-
> plications. There was the *drag* of his *indecisions*, the fine
> snapping now and again of her minor *relinquishments*.
> Her health, his temperament, their varying poverty — they

were delayed, deflected. She was *ordered* abroad for successive winters, to places he could not expect to endure.

It hits off a flaccid type, as it is intended to.

This use of grammar is pervasive for all the characters. "She gave so little answer to one's enquiry that one did not know how to approach." The impersonal pronoun is more than neutral. It is as chilling as an astral emanation. Lois excusing herself says, as if she were talking about somebody else, "Panic is beyond one." Here are passive, impersonal, and that house which has more life than any of them all together in two sentences: "Lois *was sent* upstairs for the shawls; *it appeared* that a touch of dew on the bare skin might be fatal. . . . On the bare stairs *her feet found their* evening echoes; she dawdled, listening." Again, in a lovely run of moods and images, when they are all seated outside on the steps:

> Turning half around, she watched light breathe through the tips of the cigarettes; it seemed as though everybody were waiting. Night now held the trees with a toneless finality. The sky shone, whiter than glass, fainting down to the fretted leaf-line, but was being steadily drained by the dark below, to which the grey of the lawns, like smoke, as steadily mounted. The house was highest of all with toppling immanence like a cliff.

It is a most effective scene: the beleaguered party chatting lightly, at rest, in the summer evening, under the tall façade of the house, until, suddenly, they hear the sound of a patrolling lorry, furtive, sinister, "like some one running and crouching behind a hedge." They retire, closing the doors for the night on the impersonal danger.

This fabulous atmosphere as of people under a spell, as marmoreal as a halted procession, fits the theme of this novel perfectly. This was their very last autumnal stay in that house. Fatality was in the offing. But fatality is always in the offing. In *To the North* Markie Linkwater — another favored type of Miss Bowen's, the near cad — is literally thrown into Cecilia Summers's lap: a jolting train brings them together in a dining car. She had wished to be alone. As for him, he "never asked more of women than affability; intimacy was shocking to him." She is "mistrustful, tentative, uncertain." Identically, her friend Emmeline had never wanted to become intimate with Julian Summers. Myopic, overserious, she has so far spent her years "watching slip past her a blurred repetitive pattern she took to be life." Once, indeed, she had been kissed by a sailor on a battleship while looking up at Orion through a pair of opera glasses, which he knocked out of her hand when he grabbed her. "Since the sailor she seemed to have been surrounded by shadowy people, acting without impulse, with no spring of passion in their behaviour, not throwing cracked opera-glasses as he did into the sea."

As for Julian, he is without vitality, prefers inexact desires, is speculative and recessive. Once when another of Miss Bowen's favored types, the demon child, the *Backfisch* at the lacy-drawers stage, is foisted on him for a week he suffers agonies of self-consciousness in her company. He sees that the poor child's approximation to what she thinks is naturalness is a parody of his own artificiality. She makes him feel as if somebody had scrubbed him clean, and all society becomes "a Turkish bath peopled by nudes." From her Julian flies to Cecilia for comfort: to be with her was to be in "dazzling ignorance of oneself," shrouded in an illusion of affection.

One may well imagine that such unenterprising types are less likely to step into the line of fate than to be drawn by its magnet. Their only hope of safety is to remain indoors. Even Saint John's Wood is a grave risk for such stay-at-home Red Riding Hoods. Wolves must be provided. That is the function of the near cad. When he attaches himself to Emmeline he blinds her: she gives herself to him utterly. Unprepared for hazards, how could she be expected to know the ropes? Her passion frightens him. He wants to pull out. Doomed and joyless victim, she kills herself and him in a wild motor drive at night to the Pole Star — *To the North.*

It is not, then, just one woman or two who move in the light of the fable. They are all touched by the spell. They all disguise under a mask of determination their interior surrender to the pressures of fate. One of Miss Bowen's least assured novels is *Friends and Relations;* it is one of her most revealing for the critic. Here Janet Studdert is introduced to us on the fourth page as "a heavy-lidded and rather sombre Diana," supervising the Wolf Cubs at her sister's wedding. Her sister marries one Edward Tilney, the son of Lady Elfrida Tilney, who had been divorced for adultery with a big-game hunter named Considine Meggatt of Batts Monachorum, a landed gentleman. Janet remains heavy-lidded and sombre throughout the book, but not at all Dianesque; indeed, as we gradually realize that she is the "heroine" we begin to observe that, far from being a huntress, she is being firmly propelled, half awake, half aware, like a beautiful white cow to some sacrificial altar somehow or other connected with her sister's marriage and with the big-game hunter. We see this when she becomes engaged, only six weeks after her sister's wedding, to the nephew of the wicked big-game hunter, Rodney Meggatt; for after many pages, many hints and ten years, it transpires that she had all along cherished a tender feeling for her sister's husband, Edward Tilney, and that he had cherished a tender feeling for her. She has — which is, to say the very least, highly extravagant and fanciful on her part — married the big-game hunter's nephew Rodney because this brings her vaguely into Edward Tilney's life on the slim ground that it was the wicked big-game hunter's affair with Lady Elfrida that broke Edward's childhood in two. This elaborate device to indicate the mesmeric nature of the force which governs Janet's will reveals to us the lengths to which Miss Bowen will go to deprive her characters of their autonomy.

"Early," she writes of the mesmerized Janet, "while her hair was still down her back she had accepted maturity; as though someone touching on her shoulder had told her to come away before the party had begun." To grow up is to submit to forces felt as inimical. Perhaps a week later, Janet still unmarried, we are told: "These last weeks she had noticed someone who was herself for the first time, she could see nothing nowadays but herself, *a figure she watched with fatalism.*" Ten years later an unpleasant young woman who had observed the course of all those concerned in those two marriages wonders whether, somewhere, sometime, Janet made a decision between a glance at and a glance away from Edward, and from that moment "they both lived on *involuntarily.*" Even when at long last she emerges from her trancelike state and faces the present and the past, we are told that "with impassive docility she lent herself to the retrospect." She faces the future in a similar mood, and she makes Edward see it in that mood, and as she speaks "she bends her head and looks into the palm of her hand like a sibyl."

It begins to appear that what is happening in all these stories is a clash between two aspects of life more easy to feel than to define. This bifrontal novelist sees life as two opposing forces. Shall we think of the clash as between innocence and knowledge? Youth and maturity? The dream and the actuality? Romance and that ordinary which we tend to call reality? The wish to be heroic and the nature of things, which defeats heroism? Or the wish for peace and the desire for the battle? Certainly these unmotivated people seem to be drawn out of their safe harborages by hypnotizing fingers that they cannot resist. But just as the hypnotist cannot persuade his subject to act contrary to his subject's basic nature and basic will, we must believe that these people do not resist the hypnotizing fingers only because they do not want to resist hard enough. They have at least some impulse to revolt. Somewhere beyond the enclosing piers, the familiar lighthouse, beyond the moaning bar they feel that there is something more worth while than where and as they are. They are timid, but the pull is irresistible because, after all, it is within themselves, a power more elemental, more primordial than anything they have been taught or think they think. Night after night one or two of the marooned hear from far out beyond the lighthouse the old atavistic sirens call above the whisper of the ooze and the drip of the town's sewer water. The pub lights of the harbor are appealing, the galley is warm, people are playing bridge in the lighted villas on the hill, the Palais de Dance is neon red, the radio is Light Programme. Yet, sooner or later a dark figure fumbles at a rope and puts out a boat. She will never return.

These novels are exquisitely composed logs of disaster, full of tender understanding, pity, and admiration for courage. They are also ruthless in their truth. With a sad *mouchoir* Miss Bowen waves her heroines over the cataract she has prepared for them. This is sad — because these young people are not Emma Bovarys asking for impossible experiences. They ask only for the simplest things — honest feeling, sympathy, trust, love. Is one to understand that these things are unattainable in modern society? If so, what, one asks, has gone wrong? It is pretty much the question that all these writers of the twenties* ask and answer, each in his own way. One could consider Miss Bowen as a tragic obverse of Evelyn Waugh.

Nowhere is the clash more explicitly and movingly stated than in *The Death of the Heart,* surely her best novel. The period is the late thirties. Thomas and Anna Quayne are a childless couple, aged about thirty-six and thirty-four. They are prosperous; they have three servants, live in an urban stucco house facing Regent's Park, could be envied, should be happy. One cannot, however, escape the effect of the words chosen in the opening pages to describe the sort of desirable Regency house in which they live:

> At the far side of the road dusk set the Regency buildings back at a *false* distance: against the sky they were

* *The Last September* is placed in the years 1920 and 1921. *Friends and Relations:* Part One is dated "192–"; Part Two is ten years later. *To the North* is not dated but is clearly post-1918. In *The Death of the Heart* Thomas Quayne and his wife Anna were born in 1900 and 1902, or within a year one side or the other of those dates. Stella of *The Heat of the Day* is "a year or two younger than the century." They are all people who came to their majorities in the twenties.

colourless silhouettes, insipidly ornate, *brittle and cold.* The
blackness of windows not yet lit or curtained made the
houses look *hollow inside.*

Thomas's father, an idealistic, sentimental old buffer,
would have been just up Mr. Waugh's street — the typical,
futile, fumbling bourgeois who would sign Peace Pledges
every week and would in a couple of years be acclaiming
Mr. Chamberlain, and probably behave like a brave man
under the bombs. At the age of fifty-seven he had committed
adultery with a fluffy young widow named Irene and, much
to his dismay, been cheerfully packed off to the Continent
with her by his wife. Irene bore a child, Portia, now an
orphan, aged sixteen. She has been sent to stay with Thomas
and Anna by her dying father. "He had felt," Anna explains
dryly to a friend, "that Portia had grown up exiled not only
from her own country but from normal, cheerful family
life." She adds, uncomfortably, that "he idealised us rather,
you see." (Symbolists may decide why the child was called
Portia. She does seem to sit in judgment on Thomas and
Anna, in her lonely and agonizing longing for "normal,
cheerful family life," her "impossible lovingness and austere
trust.") And yet these two must have seemed wholly normal to everybody else. We have met them thousands of times,
an upright, well-meaning, refined couple, eager to be kind
and civilized towards everyone. The child's hunger for affection is too much for them; too much for that brittle, cold,
colorless, hollow house that they think of as a home, "shut-
tered and muffled" against the noise of the city, where the
lamplight binds the room "in unreal circles," where the
heart shines only with the sterile glow of an electric fire. (I
am, of course, translating, and therefore destroying the

subtle suggestiveness of an artist who uses her words with the most delicate implications. She does not say any of these things. They pass imperceptibly into us as part of the poignant mood she elicits, touch after touch, from our sensibilities. The only criticism one might make is that she does make her characters feel at a higher level than their own sensibilities. But does this matter?)

In the end Portia feels betrayed by everybody except the dour old family servant Matchett, who though dour is still "natural." She is betrayed especially by Eddie, the near cad, whom she is drawn to love, or to imagine she loves, but who pities her rather than loves her, seeing in her another victim of the world he also, but more frankly, fears and hates and tries to be spry enough to cope with. There can be no question as to what these two young people symbolize. They, though primarily Portia, represent an excess of innocence that, with a foolhardiness possible only in the pure of heart, constantly affronts what Miss Bowen significantly calls "the system of our affections," which is "too corrupt" for innocence and therefore shatters it. In this world where life is always "edited" (her word) by this corrupt system anything which is unedited is doomed. "Why," Eddie says passionately to Portia — and it is a cry which all the writers of the twenties, and since, assume to be justified — "why should we be at the start of our two lives when everything around us is losing its virtue? How can we grow up when there's nothing left to inherit, when what we have to feed on is stale and corrupt?" And when Thomas is made to think that "society was self-interest given a pretty gloss," a web of calculation where only love, he hoped, was uncalculated, we have to see that by love he does not mean charity but merely an emotion likewise centered on himself, or at most on one other person. There is no place in such a world for Portia, for anybody so "thorough," so absolute, so honest.

Even Eddie, her fellow odd-man-out, cannot put up with her absoluteness. In exasperation he says to her towards the end, "You expect every bloody thing to be right or wrong, and to be done with the whole of oneself." And, "All the other women I've known but you, Portia, seem to know what to expect, and that gives me something to go on. I don't care how wrong they are: it gets one along." Again, "Because I said I loved you you expect me to be as sweet to you as my mother. You're damned lucky to have somebody even as innocent as I am." Inevitably we begin to see the joke of it all. Portia is so tragic that she becomes comic. Young acquaintances tell her she is bats. A twist of the globe and, like her papa, she would be a figure for Evelyn Waugh. But by another twist she and Eddie would be fit for Graham Greene, another Rose, another Pinkie. And indeed such innocence as hers has to be thought "bats" by this workaday world of ours or we are all either bats or criminals, as we possibly are whenever we are being worldly. The force of this book is that it says, firmly, "Choose!" It puts things up to us. It is at the same time an enormous tribute to Miss Bowen's sense of proportion, as well as to her technical skill in wisely lowering the temperature for a while, that she can, for a whole central stretch of the novel, overlay the subject with a humor that never diminishes our sympathy with Portia, never allows us to forget that hearts break every day with a grin.

Let us call the clash a clash between the world and the blind values of unspoiled youth. These novels are written in sorrowing admiration, perhaps even in envy, of youth, that age of dreams when alone truth is whole and faith is utter and hopes are unbroken and love is perfect, that age which is so "impossible" to us elders, when love is impossibly romantic, too dramatic, misled, misplaced, hopelessly exaggerated — and which leads to fatality whenever adults try to live out their youthful honesty in this inimical social world. Miss Bowen is all on the side of what youth believes, but she is a worldly woman, and she knows that it does not work, and her characters have to pay for her pleasure in wishing that it might work. Like Flaubert she is relentless in the end. She differs from him only as an Irishwoman's sentiment differs from a Frenchman's intelligence, so that she sighs more audibly as she snaps the frail threads of hopeless innocence.

In *The House in Paris* the following revealing passage suggests an *idée maîtresse:*

> . . . young girls like the excess of any quality. Without knowing it they want to suffer, to suffer they must exaggerate; they like to have loud chords struck on them. Loving art better than life they need men to be actors; only an actor moves them, with his telling smile, undomestic, out of touch with the everyday that they dread. They love to enjoy love as a system of doubts and shocks. They are right: not seeking husbands yet they have no reason to see love socially. This natural fleshly protest against good taste is broken down soon enough; their natural love of the cad is outwitted by their mothers. Vulgarity, inborn like original sin, unfolds with the woman nature, unfolds ahead of it quickly and has a flamboyant flowering in the young girl.

There are many of these young girls in Miss Bowen's novels, these flamboyant roses, overgrown, "vulgar," undomestic, not giving a damn about worldly good taste, over-romantic, passionate in a leggy way, rebelliously indifferent to love as Mamma sees it, suffering, and adept at making others suffer too; young monsters, as they seem to us weary, middle-aged, self-cosseting elders who have long since forgotten the miseries of our youth. It is only when we see them lacerating themselves that we remember, and thank God that the beastly business of being young is over. They are Theodora and Dorothea in *Friends and Relations,* Pauline in *To the North,* Henrietta in *The House in Paris.* (Leopold, in the same novel, is a male counterpart, and he is more of a girl than a boy — but I do not think Miss Bowen knows about boys as she does about girls.) They appear in many of the short stories. The girl in "The Parrot" will grow up to be one of these vulgarians. She will grow up to suffer. For it is these girls who grow up to be Miss Bowen's doomed heroines. They still enjoy love for its shocks and doubts. They have a weakness for the cad. They exaggerate, do not seek husbands, refuse to think socially. The large question, indeed, about the Bowenesque heroine is whether she is ever truly adult. Carnally and sentimentally her women are incontinently involved in the toils of their own adolescence. They go on dreaming too long. So Karen, in *The House in Paris,* thinks when she has crossed her line of fate that this is something that should have happened long ago, and seems to think too that now she can, having poured the libation, return to her normal life. She says to her lover, "You and I are the dream." He promptly kills himself.

Elizabeth Bowen is a romantic up against the despotism of reality. So are many other Irish writers. The metallic brilliance, even the occasional jarring brassiness and jauntiness

of her style are, in an admirable sense, fake, a deceptive cocoon wrapped about the central precious, tender thing. One
could imagine a hare settling into her form, a sticky little
leveret between her paws, or perhaps a lioness growling over
her young. It is the growl of *Ich grolle nicht,* the Flaubertian
coldness imposed on Irish feeling, and the theme is so heart-
breaking that it would be embarrassing if she were not tight-
lipped about those heroines who just do not know what
o'clock it is once love enters their unwary lives. She writes of
romantic heroines in an age that has made the two words
pejorative. The underlying assumptions here are very much
of the twenties. The conflicts are no longer clear enough to
justify bold affirmations, positive statements of loyalty,
straight fights or declared aims or ends. Miss Bowen's heroines are, after all, always defeated. In Mauriac's phrase, their
beauty is borrowed from despair. Not, as we have seen, that
Miss Bowen is antiheroic, but she must state coldly that heroism, the absolute aim, does not stand a chance in modern
society, even while she still insists passionately that it is always worth trying for. She has not assumed that we must
therefore reject tradition, but she is plainly unenthusiastic
about it. She does not assume that violence is the only possible alternative in fiction to thought. She does not assume that
the intellect must be abdicated by the modern novelist. She
hovers patiently over her subjects. But the prime technical
characteristic of her work, as of other modern women writers,
such as Virginia Woolf, is that she fills the vacuum which the
general disintegration of belief has created in life by the
pursuit of sensibility. It is a highly sophisticated pursuit.
Sometimes it is overconscious and overdone.

Her sensibility can be witty; it can also be catty, even

brassy, too smart, like an overclever décor for a ballet. I do
not mind that it is, to my taste, on occasion vulgar, though
not quite in the sense in which her young girls are vulgar.
She has defended, or at least pleaded for sympathy with,
vulgarity, and are there not times when good taste is itself a
little vulgar? One thinks of the ghastly good taste of Mr.
Charles Morgan. But what one means by finding this kind of
good taste rather vulgar is that it is bloodless, and that one
longs occasionally for a good, warm, passionate howl like that
of an Italian mother baying over her dead child. This sort of
earthiness is outside the range of any English-trained writer.
When Elizabeth Bowen is dealing with elemental things she
skirts around them with too much elegance. There are certain
things she will not deign to describe. The actual falling in
love of her people is one. So that if one feels that tragedy is a
race where one has to take one's fences, must one not feel that
there is a bit too much dressage about *The Heat of the Day?*

The one occasion she is really earthy is when she is
being humorous, and would, many times over, that she were
humorous more often, for when she is being humorous she is
also most human. Louie in *The Heat of the Day* is not only
good fun but real, down to earth; far more so than Robert,
Harrison and Stella pirouetting about each other exhaust-
ingly. Yet, to take a fair measure of the humanity (as against
the elegance) of her sensibilities, one may compare them
with the sensibilities of Virginia Woolf, whose antennae are
as sensitive as remote radar, but who reacts not so much to
human beings as to things and "states of mind." Miss Bowen
is also responsive to things and states of mind, but she responds chiefly, and warmly, to her own favored types of people. "Things," Mrs. Woolf characteristically makes Terence

Hewitt say in *The Voyage Out*, "things I feel come to me like lights. I want to combine them. Have you ever seen fireworks that make figures? I want to make figures." That also, to my taste, is a form of vulgarity through elegance. Miss Bowen would never be quite so refined. She wants to make people not figures, to put them into conflict with society, and her explorations of their feelings are never just an exploitation of her own.

Her outer-imposed limitations do, nevertheless, obtrude themselves. *The Death of the Heart* was, indeed, a firm and passionately felt protest against the modern desiccation of feeling, but one could not help noting that it offered no moral approach to the problem: meaning that it intimated no norm to set against the subnormal. But can one reasonably blame Miss Bowen for this? We are brought back by this longing for a norm to the death of the traditional Hero, that symbol of the norm in all traditional literature. She, too, can only present us with the Martyr in place of the Hero, the representative not of the norm but of the disease. Greene's alternative is God. Miss Bowen is too deeply rooted in the great, central humanist tradition of European culture to take refuge in hereafters. What she directs our eyes towards is the malady of our times that breaks the dreaming and gallant few. It is what her master Flaubert did with Emma Bovary, more ruthlessly. She has described the dilemma of our times honestly, beautifully and at times movingly. To have done so much, and done it so well, is to have done a great deal.

VIRGINIA WOOLF
and JAMES JOYCE

Narcissa and Lucifer

SINCE Joyce was born in 1882, published *Chamber Music* in 1907, *Dubliners* in 1914, *A Portrait of the Artist as a Young Man* in 1916, and *Ulysses* in 1922, he has no place chronologically among a group of writers who came to their majorities in the twenties. *Ulysses* must, however, have had a large influence on the period, and I suspect that even Virginia Woolf, who disliked it, was not unaffected by its technique when writing *The Waves* and *Between the Acts*. But I am putting the two together for other reasons. I think it may be profitable to contrast Mrs. Woolf's "moments of vision" with Joyce's "epiphanies"; to compare his metaphysical view of reality with her rather simpler viewpoint; and to place both in the tradition of individualistic revolt against the order of nature and society which is so evident in all fiction in our time. I am also collocating these two writers in order to force a question which I have held back until this last essay, and which, putting it very simply, is to ask whether any literature can be in health and vigor without some form of faith.

To explain what I mean by faith I will begin by quoting from Mr. Richard Blackmur's essay on "The Later Poetry of Yeats" from his volume *The Expense of Greatness:*[*]

> Poetry does not flow from thin air but requires always a literal faith, an imaginative faith, or, as in Shakespeare, a mind full of provisional faiths. The life we all live is not alone enough of a subject for a serious artist; it must be life with a leaning, life with a tendency to shape itself only in certain forms, to afford its most lucid revelations only in certain lights. If our final interest, both as poets and as readers, is in the reality declared when the forms have been removed and the lights taken away, yet we never come to the reality at all without the first advantage of the forms and the lights. Without them we should see nothing, but only glimpse something unstable. . . . So it was with the early Yeats; his early poems are fleeting, some of them beautiful and some that sicken, as you read them, to their own extinction. But as he acquired for himself a discipline, however unacceptable to the bulk of his readers, his poetry obtained an access of reality. . . . It is almost the mark of the poet of genuine merit in our time . . . that he performs his work in the light of an insight, a group of ideas, and a faith, with the discipline that flows from them, which, taken together, form a view of life which most readers cannot share, and which, furthermore, most readers feel as repugnant, or sterile, or simply inconsequential. All this is to say . . . that our culture is incomplete with regard to poetry.

[*] *The Expense of Greatness.* New York, 1940, p. 75.

Clearly, Mr. Blackmur does not mean, as I certainly do not
mean, by faith any schematized set of dogmatic beliefs held,
or expected to be held, by a mass of people in common. Indeed, the essay points out that Yeats could write in a state of
exaltation unrelated to any concord or system ("All Souls
Night"), as he could exploit bare emotion without reference
to character ("A Deep Sworn Vow"); and it further stresses
that poetry may rely on evanescent conventions. The example Mr. Blackmur gives is not *Othello,* but it could well
have been in so far as jealousy in our time is not, apart from
certain unregenerate Latin countries, as powerfully savage
and elemental an emotion as it once was. The burthen of the
essay is the constructional use that Yeats made of the political and mythological hieroglyphics, or forms, offered to him
by Ireland; and it concerns itself, over all, with the super-
structure he built for his emotions out of magical lore. A
faith, then, for literary purposes, means any feeling for life
or any way of seeing life which is coherent, persistent, inclusive and forceful enough to give organic form to the totality
of a writer's work.

To apply this, I doubt if anybody who has studied the
totality of Virginia Woolf's work can have failed to sense
that, for all its manifold flashes of acute feeling, her abid-
ing weakness was her inability — of which she herself was
not unaware — so to feel life, so to write about it that form
would grow into her work as a child's bones grow into the
original frail embryo conceived in passion.

When, in art, the word is made flesh it is also made bone.
"The idea," Flaubert thought, "is born of the form." It
would seem to me more reasonable to say that form is born
of the idea, or that the idea can only express itself in form,

but the two, Flaubert rightly felt, are inseparable. It is as if the concept which strikes the artist takes flesh in his mind in terms of shapes which, in turn, impress themselves on his page or his canvas, and are then the apparently inevitable organic expression of his first emotion. They are coincident or congruent with it. This apparently inevitable organic form is, I must insist on thinking, quite different from the stuck-on form of *Ulysses*, where the classical reference is either a technical preconception or a postrationalization, except in so far as Bloom and Stephen may, possibly, have been felt from the beginning as a classical father-in-search-of-son theme. And, even so, is the form not apparent as something forced on, rather than emergent from, the material itself? On the other hand, the form of Faulkner's *Light in August* is organic form. It was inherent. It has all the appearances of inevitability. One does not feel that the dual myth, of Cain and Babel, was chosen, preconceived, rationally imposed. It has all the appearances of having arisen in Faulkner's imagination simultaneously with whatever passing experience in actual life excited him to start writing. In that flash he conceived a theme and it, literally, took shape. By contrast, when I say that *For Whom the Bell Tolls* leaves no clear arc behind it in the sky of the mind I mean that Hemingway had not fully realized what he wanted his experience to mean.

Form and meaning, then, or form and faith (in the sense in which I have understood faith) are very close to one another. Form is a descent of the Holy Ghost on the soul ready to receive it. It is an epiphany, a manifestation, a showing-forth, a tongue of fire, after which the apostle can speak "in divers tongues the wonderful works of God." In literature the descent can come from pure genius, a lightning flash of intuition when we see into the souls of things; or it can come, more painfully, through a combination of intelligence and sensibility when an artist winds his way into the heart of his subject. In the one event, as with Wordsworth, the result may be the gradual development of a growing, and possibly integrated, body of faith — again in our sense of that word. Examples of the second process range from Ben Jonson to Conrad, from Donne to Eliot: a faith — again in the literary sense — brought to bear on the subject so deliberately, so willfully that it is often the writer's business to give the opposite impression, to conceal, that is, his a priori slant or attitude.

Now, if Mrs. Woolf so rarely achieved organic form I suggest that the reason is that she was unable to deduce "an insight, a group of ideas" from her experience of life. She remained to the end so intoxicated by the wonder-making variety of the universe that she never achieved a position of intellectual or emotional equipoise in relation to outer reality, and so never won control over herself or over her material. She never constructed her faith. She never achieved form. Moore said that Pater's meaning was often lost in the folds of his style. Mrs. Woolf's ultimate meaning is constantly lost in the folds of her sensibility, and of her narcissism.

But we must not use terms like "reality," "control," "constructed," or "sensibilities" without some effort at definition.

I write these pages in a room which has a bay window of four sections. If I rise from my desk and look out through the left-hand section, I may record in my mind that "I see the quadrangle." I do not, in fact, see the quadrangle. I see only a portion of it. What I see, furthermore, is a portion of the quad isolated within the frame of this section of my window.

This frame encloses a form of picture — the tower, a tree, some grass, some stone, some windows, a student who has paused and is reading a letter, a segment of the sky and some clouds. Since all these things are artificially related to one another by being framed, I not only see those various things but am aware of their pictorial relationship, which changes them from facts to forms, eloquent now through their relationship. Moreover, I am aware of certain memories and associations that they evoke. Thus, when the hot-water pipes clink, these related shapes, inexplicably, cause me to imagine that I hear a blacksmith's anvil in an Irish village many miles away. (Proust went fully into this aspect of vision.) Much else that I remember, though I do not explicitly define my memories, is part of my experience as I look out of my window "at the quadrangle." For my outward glance has by this time become an emotional experience. Patently, if I wished to record the essence of this slight experience I could not put it all in, as, often, Mrs. Woolf so passionately wished she could. I must select, as she fully realized and said. The crucial question arises: By what canon do I select?

Consider, for example, alone, how far time is involved, time which involves knowledge, not merely springing from my own personal memories but from racial and atavistic memories that are every man's inheritance, and which willy-nilly become part of that minute experience of looking from my study window. Vision, it seems, then, is not alone a sensory or emotional experience; it is also an intellectual decision, or choice, or selection, in response to the invitation or challenge of what we see. No experience can be otherwise, since it is, in effect, part of that perpetual process of wedding the subject (I) with the object (the Not I), unless, by

some fierce negation akin to barbarism, a man blots out
whole portions of his intellectual being. (Faulkner seems to
have managed to do this.) This wedding, this interfusion,
this suture, a copenetrative process like the sexual act, sometimes spoken of as "knowing" a woman, alerts within us a
communication with the significance embedded in outer
reality which is, in the ultimate, a participation in some essence common to both the person who experiences and the
mode of his experience. It is for this essence that we are always seeking, selectively; the element common to the thing
and to us; that which, as we say, makes the thing meaningful
to us. We exist in ourselves, that is, only when we have existed in others. We do not hold the mirror up to nature.
Nature holds the mirror up to us.

> For speculation turns not to itself
> Until it hath travelled and is mirrored there
> Where it may see itself.

I am insisting, it will be seen, that every artist's communication with life is not only an emotional and intellectual act
but a moral act. It is what Simone Weil said of all created
beauty: it is an entry into the mouth of the labyrinth at
whose center (in her symbolism) God is waiting to eat us up;
or, in more secular language, at whose core we are merged
with the mystery, or meaning, of all life, all reality, and in
some degree partake of it — unless, to be sure, we are writing best sellers.

Now, in her own way, Mrs. Woolf acknowledged and asserted all this. The end of the journey, she saw, is certainly
not just photographic or naturalistic reproduction. Realism,
as the word goes, for its own pure or impure sake was, to her,

just "waste." But how far did she realize that when outer reality is inwardly re-created it becomes hypostasized? Into what it is changed nobody can say, but changed it is. Proust would say that it is distilled into essences, and a Thomist could probably find common ground with him, saying that the end of all art is reached when the artist has so played about with the accidents of experience as to reveal its essence. But these are no more than wordy efforts to express our awareness of the change. My feeling is that Mrs. Woolf fell into the very impasse she detested: that she did not change her experience at all, but that she did record and reproduce most delicately, yet quite naturalistically, the externals of life.

It is indeed true that the fleshly envelope of life which she wished to dissolve, to make luminous, becomes often much less opaque than it had been — this we gratefully acknowledge — yet it remains as she found it. That "access of reality" which came to the later Yeats as he achieved a form of discipline, "in the light of an insight, a group of ideas, and a faith . . . a view of life," continued to evade her. And this is why, finally, I have spoken of her sensibilities and her narcissism; because I think that she was too absorbed in her private self to wed experience fully. She could not give herself utterly. It always happens when our sensibilities are too hotly pursued. The subject (or ego) is overemphasized; the object is underemphasized; the enemy lying in wait is subjectivity.

It is fascinating, and sometimes depressing, to watch her groping with this only half-understood problem. When writing *The Waves,* which she originally intended to call *The Moths,* she wrote in her *Diary:*

I mean to eliminate all waste, deadness, superfluity, to give the moment whole; whatever it includes. Say that the moment is a combination of thought, sensation, the voice of the sea. Waste, deadness, come from the inclusion of things that don't belong to the moment; this appalling narrative business of the realist; getting on from lunch to dinner; it is false, unreal, merely conventional. Why admit anything to literature that is not poetry, by which I mean saturated? Is that not my grudge against the novelists? That they select nothing? The poets succeeded by simplifying; practically everything is left out. I want to put practically everything in: yet to saturate. That is what I want to do in *The Moths*. It must include nonsense, fact, sordidity, but made transparent.

Four pages after deciding "to put practically everything in" she decided: "I shall do away with exact place and time. Anything may be out of the window — a ship — a desert — London."

She had only momentary realizations of the fact that her real enemy was herself, that she was caught in the individualist's impasse of what, in the following passage, she calls "the damned egotistical self." One could ponder long on the misconceptions of this entry in her *Diary*. I italicize the phrases which arrest me:

This afternoon arrived at some idea of a new form for a new novel. Suppose one thing should open out of another — as in an unwritten novel — only not for ten pages but for two hundred or so — doesn't that give the looseness and lightness I want? Doesn't that get closer and yet keep *form* and speed, and enclose everything, everything? *What the unity shall be I have yet to discover; the theme is a blank to me* . . . I suppose the danger is the damned egotistical self *which ruins Joyce and Richardson to my mind*.

This egotistical self seems very much to the fore in another entry:

> I am now and then haunted by some semi-mystic, very profound life of a woman which should all be told on one occasion; and time shall be utterly obliterated; future shall somehow blossom out of the past. One incident — say the fall of a flower — might contain it. My theory being that *the actual event practically does not exist,* nor time either.

There is one crucial passage in the *Diary.* It is, in the literal sense, one of those agnostic confessions which gives us a troubling insight into the heart of her dilemma:

> Why is there not a discovery in life? Something one could lay hands on and say, "This is it." My depression is a harassed feeling. I'm looking — but that's not it, that's not it. What is it? And I shall die before I find it? Then (as I was walking in Russell Square last night) I see the mountains in the sky; the great clouds; and the moon which is risen over Persia. I have a great and astonishing sense of something there which is "it." It's not exactly beauty that I mean. It is that the thing is in itself enough, satisfactorily achieved. A sense of my own strangeness, walking on the earth, is there too; of the infinite oddity of the human position; trotting along Russell Square with the moon up there and those mountain clouds. Who am I; what am I; and so on.

If it were not for the whole context of her life one might dismiss this as anybody's casual, mock-serious "What does it all mean?" Knowing her prevailing attitude to life, we see a sensitive, serious, delicate-minded woman, the daughter of Sir Leslie Stephen, the eminent Cambridge rationalist, who had been married to Thackeray's daughter, known almost every distinguished writer of his era — she was the god-

daughter of James Russell Lowell; Meredith is said to have
fallen in love with her when she was ten — walking in Russell Square (that is to say, looking out of *her* study window)
and not so much not knowing what she sees as not seeing it
at all. Clouds and the moon. Narcissa involved in her own
strangeness all her life. Subject and object far from at peace
with one another. The experience is certainly not intellectual, though she may think of it as "mystical." (The event
practically does not exist, or time either.) Russell Square
does not exist. It does not radiate out in associations, or into
any accepted traditions, is not firmly seated in what we must
call the forms of society, has, in short, so little sense of fixture
or solidity that the moon is over Ispahan. Certainly this
daughter of the great Victorians will not want to write novels
about any sort of real, accepted world. (She was to try it,
once, in *The Years,* a novel which almost broke her, and
which is the least characteristic of all her books, and can only
be counted a sad failure — for her.) She and where she was
could never have been a unity. No wonder she can
say, "When I write I am merely a sensibility." And add,
"Sometimes I like being Virginia, but only" — she goes on
rather disapprovingly — "when I'm scattered, and various
and gregarious."

Once she records a snatch of conversation with Lytton
Strachey:

> Strachey: And the novel?
> Virginia: Oh, I put in my hand and rummage in the
> branpie.
> Strachey: Yes, that's what's so wonderful, and it's all dif-
> ferent!
> Virginia: Yes, I'm twenty people.

What order, form, method, meaning, significance, one must wonder, can possibly be won by the branpie method?

Her Bloomsbury friends, one fears, were, like Strachey, much too evasive, polite and kind. But one gave her a clear pointer to her difficulty, and with her usual honesty she saw the point. When Roger Fry told her that she was overdoing the prose-lyric vein, she saw the truth and force of the criticism. "I poetise my inanimate scenes, stress my personality, *don't let the meaning emerge from the matière.*" It was the outward symptom of her inability to come to terms with actuality, to give it a fair "do," to cut down her ration of "personality." Here, for example, is an allegedly prose passage describing a woman (Mrs. Dalloway) sewing by the window of her home in London (I print it for what it really is — vers libre):

> *Quiet descended on her, calm, content, as her needle,*
> *Drawing the silk smoothly to its gentle pause,*
> *Collected the green folds together,*
> *And attached them very lightly to the belt.*
> *So, on a summer's day,*
> *Waves collect, overbalance and fall;*
> *Collect and fall;*
> *And the whole world seems to be saying, that is all,*
> *More and more ponderously,*
> *Until even the heart in the body which lies in the sun*
> *On the beach says too, that is all.*
> *Fear no more, says the heart.*
> *Fear no more, says the heart, committing its burthen*
>   *to some sea*
> *Which sighs collectively*
> *For all sorrows,*
> *And renews, begins, collects, lets fall.*
> *And the body alone listens to the passing bee.*

"Have I the power of conveying the true reality? Or do I write essays about myself?" Her self-questioning is ruthless. And she did not always write essays about herself. There were many blessed moments, a great many, when she did humbly bed with common things and in forgetting herself in their arms revealed herself as well as them:

> The snow, which had been falling all night, lay at three o'clock in the afternoon over the field and the hill. Clumps of withered grass stood out upon the hill-top; the furze-bushes were black, and now and then a black shiver crossed the snow as the wind drove flurries of frozen particles before it. The sound was of a broom sweeping — sweeping.

That is nature holding the mirror up to the artist: a beautiful picture of Virginia Woolf. It is an enchanting pause set in the flow of life, like standing on a steppingstone for a second to glance at the stream at one's feet, a brief, of necessity brief, moment of personal ecstasy, a summary of, a purification of the perpetual flux of common things.

What did Virginia Woolf, in the broadest possible sense of the word, "believe" in terms of the most provisional "faith"? I think she believed chiefly, like all that Cambridge set who were her friends, in the revelatory possibilities of "states of mind."

Recall her first novel, *The Voyage Out*. Helen and Ridley Ambrose, Clarissa and Richard Dalloway, and Rachel Vinrace, the Ambroses' niece, are on a ship bound for a resort in South America. Throughout Mrs. Woolf seems to speak through her characters. So, Rachel, a young idealist, much bewildered by the ways of the world, when kissed by Dalloway is assured that "the common fleshly reality of all this is insignificant." She will meet Terence Hewett in San Marina and form an attachment so high-minded that it will come to nothing. Thus, when they see another pair of lovers kissing, Terence says, "Their lives are now changed for ever." Rachel says, "I could almost burst into tears." Terence says, "There's something horribly pathetic about it, I agree." (This could be funny, but it is not meant to be.) Terence wants to write a novel about silence; that is, about the things people do not say. He says:

"What I want to do in writing novels is very much what you want to do when you play the piano. . . . We want to find out what's behind things, don't we? Look at the lights down there scattered about anyhow. Things, I feel, come to me like lights. I want to combine them. I want to make figures." (Which is very much what the author so often seems to be doing.)

He again seems to speak for her when he says, "There's no difficulty in conceiving incidents; the difficulty is to put them into shape — not to get run away with." Or, when uttering a preference for writing about the past, he says that it detaches one from modern conditions so that one can make one's characters "more abstract than people who live as we do." Rachel, I feel, is also reflecting her author when she says, "Does it ever seem to you, Terence, that the world is composed entirely of vast blocks of matter and that we're nothing but patches of light?"

How acute E. M. Forster was when he said that he liked this book not for its people but because it was "vague and universal." In fact, he did not like the characters; but then he "felt no need to care for them." The adjectives are just: the book is one long series of vague and universal "states of mind" in which common lives become so many "patches of light." In the end when Mrs. Woolf gives her heroine an infection of which she dies we feel that our pleasure in common life — in the young girl's voyage out into the world, her early love, her youthful discoveries — is cruelly and wantonly smacked in the face. In the last sentence the despised order of common life is sent, almost contemptuously, on its routine way — the old people in the hotel "picking up their books, their cards, their balls of wool, their workbaskets, and passing [him] one after another on their way to bed."

With her background and upbringing, surrounded by a highly intellectual, cultured, kindly, civilized but, in the end, rather drearily rationalist set, it is hard to see what Mrs. Woolf could have believed in except some such concept of life as a chimera lit by moments of sensory joy. The sound of the snow like a broom sweeping, sweeping . . . steamers in a fog resounding like gigantic tuning forks . . . cabbage leaves in the moonlight . . . memories coming back and back like a sleeper jolting against one in a railway carriage . . .

She was at her best in *The Waves* and *Between the Acts*, for two totally opposite reasons. In her last novel she found one solution for her problem of subjective involvement — comedy. In *The Waves* she virtually abandoned all effort at objectivity or detachment. She let the subjective reins fall loosely on the neck of her Pegasus and wrote a frank elegy on innocence and idealism. If one wishes to enjoy *The Waves* one should go at once from the first section, where the children are playing, to the last section, which explicitly gives the key to the many revealing, or would-be revealing, moments too lightly touched as they fall throughout the body of the story. "We had lost," says the extrovert and gregarious Bernard, "what they had kept." One may skip the stuck-on interludes about the waves: these are feeble efforts to simulate form.

At bottom, her trouble was one to which she was fully alive. "Who thinks it? And am I outside the thinker?"

It was a proper question for a novelist; it is not, we should point out to those who sometimes try to turn her into a prose poet, a proper question for a poet. The seer and the seen are on quite another plane from the thinker and the thought. A poet may do what a novelist may not do, so lose himself in the natural world that the natural world seems to be speaking with its own voice, its own life, its own mind: as in, say, Blake's *The Book of Thel* when the daughter of the Seraphim speaks:

Art thou a Worm, image of weakness, art thou but a Worm?
I see thee like an infant wrapped in the Lilly's leaf.

Such a self-merging, so direct a self-identification, with so unmediated a presence as the result, are not possible in prose, which, by reason of its function, one might say because of its mental temperature, is obliged to observe from the distance of thought or consideration. And so it becomes the urgent problem of the novelist to find out how he may experience fully and yet not surrender or evade thought, or, at least, not appear to do so, while enjoying or suffering that full experience. To revert to the sexual metaphor that I have already used more than once, if a man does not, or cannot, surrender cerebral consciousness in love he will experience not a perfect union but an incomplete union terribly close to autoeroticism; and instead of writing afterwards about total love he will be able only to write of his own isolated thoughts and sensations. From this self- or cerebral consciousness there is no release, no escape except through that abnormal duality of the novelist's mind which provides him with what Freud might call a latent censor who records in his unconscious being the nature of experiences of which at the time his consciousness makes no record at all. Long after he has left the battlefield, the gaming table, the bed, the cataract, the sociable dinner table, the river's brim, the quiet wood, the crowded street, there rise to his memory things he never remembered, words he never heard, images he never saw. His memory is partly creative because it is partly selective, because his censor is his second self, because this second self, which never sleeps, is like seeking like, incessantly. Then, with thoughtful awareness, he will reselect, arrange, shape, and by shaping state; but not until then, at the risk of an excessive subjectivity, intellectualism, devitalization, or the mere self-delineation of the narcissist locked up in his own ego.

In Joyce's work who thinks it? And is the writer outside the thinker? Does he really sit on the clouds paring his nails in godlike indifference to the doings of his characters? I suggest that he is not in the least detached, that he is, on the contrary, closely involved, both emotionally and intellectually, in the doings of all his characters. We may test this most easily by considering his first two novels.

Let us grant, to begin with, that total detachment is impossible to any writer who lives, as he must, imaginatively into his material. (Stendhal, for example, is patently woven into

all his major characters.) Grant, further, that such detachment as we think we observe, are persuaded to observe, is an
illusion on two planes. There is the illusion of unobtrusiveness
achieved by technical skill, the author's cloak of invisibility;
and there is the illusion of impartiality achieved by intellectual discipline. Now, it is plain that with Joyce the first illusion is constantly at war with the second. Far from making an
effort to persuade us that he is not present in his novels, he indicated frankly by the title of his first novel that he is his own
subject. It is true that when we first saw this novel, on its original appearance, we partially accepted the title as a sort of
double bluff, or even as a simple trick to give an illusion of
actuality; as when a novelist writes a story in the form of a
first-person diary. We could, at that date, go a long way towards accepting the flimsy disguises, make a gesture of accepting the book as purely imaginative. But *Ulysses,* and
everything we have since learned about Joyce and his techniques, put an end to that. The reader is now in the position
that he cannot tell, without much study, where autobiography ends and fiction begins.

Joyce may have foreseen this danger. For it is a danger to
persuasiveness. We do not question the imagination, we allow it great liberties, but we do question that which is not a
product of the imagination. He may well have foreseen, then,
that in putting himself into his novel he was laying a special
strain on our sympathy. He may have foreseen that we might
fear that we were being "got at" through a ventriloquist's
dummy called Stephen Daedalus. And it is true that we will
always be slow, or actually may cease, to give our assent to
any book where we feel that the characters are not autonomous but are being manipulated by a marionette master.

(This, I have indicated earlier, happens frequently with Graham Greene and Faulkner.) The result would be that we finally say to ourselves, "All right! This is how it all seemed to one highly subjective, introspective and personally involved spectator. But it is not at all necessarily the way it really was." This does not in the least detract from our pleasure; but it is, surely, not exactly the sort of pleasure Joyce proposed to give us? In any case, if we do not recognize the precise nature of our pleasure a grave misinterpretation will result.

Joyce employed three devices to give us the illusion of detachment, of objectivity. (1) He built up a realistic background by the use of a meticulously accurate naturalistic detail. (2) He used this naturalistic realism to persuade us that he was quite detached intellectually from Stephen Daedalus. I refer to the frequent use of ironical comment on Stephen through sardonic contrasts. I will give examples presently. (3) He then boldly employed the subjective method to cast the spell of Stephen's personality over us, and he did it so well that it is with the greatest difficulty that we withhold from him an entirely uncritical sympathy. Almost any sequence in which Stephen Daedalus appears will show this triple device at work. Its main purpose is always the same: to lure us into the interior of Daedalus-Joyce; once we enter that magic cave the spell becomes well-nigh irresistible. Recall the opening page of *Ulysses*.

Mulligan emerges on the roof of the martello tower at Sandycove and does some fooling with the bowl of shaving water. The whole picture is stereoscopically actual. On line twenty-six we read: "He peered sideways up and gave a long low whistle of call, then paused awhile in rapt attention, his even white teeth glistening here and there with gold points."

Still pure naturalistic actuality. Then comes the single word
"Chrysostomos." We are inside Stephen's mind. The gold fill-
ings in Mulligan's mouth have suggested to him the gold-
mouthed orator Dion Chrysostomos. Actuality now returns,
and the symphony of the interior stream is held off again until
the third page; but not until — device number two — we
have first been given a characteristic subironic picture of
Stephen with his poetic palm elegantly on his brow and
his eyes self-pityingly on his ragged sleeve, symbol of his
self-conscious poverty. Then how the violins come up! "Pain
that was not yet the pain of love fretted his heart. In sleep
she came to him." A less cunning writer might have begun
right away with that. This simple illustration of the triple
device will suffice for the moment.

We note, however, that just as Mulligan literally presents
his shaving mirror to Stephen's eyes in these opening pages
he is also, metaphorically, holding a mirror up to him for our
benefit. Stephen sees himself through or in Mulligan's eyes.
The whole saraband of characters who circle about Stephen
do likewise. He (that is, he as the mask of Joyce) oscillates
constantly between a cool observation of his fellows and a
fevered contemplation of himself. This does not make him a
Narcissus, but he is partially narcissistic in so far as he is incapable of seeing any character without relating him to himself.

Joyce's detachment, in short, is not only an illusion but, if
we are deceived by it, a delusion. We might go so far as to
call it a confidence trick which he plays on us. He was also,
no doubt, playing it on himself. "See," he says to us and to
himself, "how truthful I am about places, people, dates, details. How objective I am when I remove the mask from

Cranly, Bloom, Lister, A.E., Father Conmee, Mulligan. See
how I mock the dreams of this young fool Daedalus." We are
deeply impressed. We applaud. We fail to notice that these
characters only seem to go their own fair or unfair fleshly way
— "seem," because all the time Stephen's life is lived at the
center, reflecting them, reflected in them, turning back constantly to himself from them, self-concerned, intellectual, an
ego brooding on himself, *using* them, deploying them so as to
see and express himself in his own private world, which is, at
every moment of self-consideration, not their world but his,
the author's metaphysical subject. When this happens is
Joyce "outside the thinker"? Are we? We, too, become
part Narcissus, and the figures that shimmer in the pool
under our eyes are, for those revealing moments, no longer
objective. It is this Daedalus spell which is, in the ultimate,
the spell of the *Portrait* and *Ulysses*. While we delight in
it we must fear it. For what Joyce does is to blind us to the
fact that this is, after all, an enclosed, private and highly personal world, the envelopment of his romantic *moi*, with which
we identify ourselves. Joyce's world is not Dublin and all
that. It is as private a world as that of Proust. But Joyce, too,
is, like Proust, in search of essences, which he reveals through
what he calls epiphanies. If we were, then, to believe from
Stephen's description of his aesthetic in *Stephen Hero* that
Joyce is a classicist we would be very wide of the mark. The
amount of romanticism infused into his work by his near narcissism and exhibitionism is abundant and pervasive. Does it
matter? It matters enormously. For what we are dealing with
is a man's life sense, his view of life, his personal *manière
de voir*.

I have earlier given my definition of a novel, when dealing

with Faulkner, and must here repeat it with reference to Joyce's supposed objectivity. A novel is a prose narrative dealing with a number of characters whom the author succeeds in making interesting and persuasive, and whom he deploys in a manner that, within his view of life, he considers fitting, and we with him. The external interest of his characters is primary in point of technique; their internal interest is primary in point of importance. They are decoys, no more. We do not read about them primarily for their sake; we read about them for what the author conveys by speaking in terms of character as a painter speaks in terms of color and form. The crucial matter is the fittingness of the behavior and fate of these characters. In a novel fitness is all.

This idea or notion of fitness is purely personal to the writer if he is an individual writer, and all good modern writing has, perforce, to be individual: i.e., it does not any longer present traditional or social ideas of what is fitting. But how can we speak of fitness unless we know what sort of spectacles the writer wears? This is more or less what Mlle. Magny means when she says in *Les Sandales d'Empédocle* that all criticism is a form of autobiography: the reader walking arm in arm with the writer and saying Yes, or No, in terms of his own experience, modifying it, enlarging it with the help of the author's spectacles. It is therefore essential to be aware of the constitutents of Joyce's, or any writer's, way of looking at life.

I am aware that those who divide art from life will not be inclined to agree. To them art is self-contained. It is a picture hung on a wall about which we can be cognizant without any exterior assistance: an unmediated impact. I can only say that I do not agree, as I do not agree that I can look out of my study window without bringing to bear on the view before me a great deal of personal, traditional and acquired knowledge. To understand a work of art it is essential to grasp, as far as we can, the artist's *manière de voir,* and for this everything may be of use: knowledge of the artist's ambience, the influences that have worked on him, his place, his period; knowledge, above all, of the nature of the man himself. Over and over again, in reading the works of Joyce, we must keep on adverting to the man.

What, then, are the outstanding *human* constituents of Joyce's subjectivity? The most striking thing in all his work is the impression he conveys of a nature torn between a painful sense of shame and an almost diabolical pride. The one postulates the other. If we glance over, say, the last hundred pages of *A Portrait of the Artist as a Young Man* we will see how often the two notes are struck in references to poverty. So, when Stephen talks to Davin in his room among the poor streets around Grantham Street, he is affected by the thought of the "starving Irish village" which is Davin's background. Leaving Davin, he is importuned by a flower seller to whom he twice says, "I have no money." At the corner of Saint Stephen's Green this moment of "discouraged poverty" is prolonged in bitter hurt by the memory of the "tawdry tribute" paid to the patriot Wolfe Tone in 1898. The whole city, past and present, seems "venal" to him, a purchasable quantity. In a characteristic contrast he enters the college and begins to discuss the nature of the beautiful with a priest while the priest is lighting a fire with parsimoniously garnered candle ends. "A desolating pity" begins "to fall on his easily embittered heart." (There may or may not be a symbol here of the materials of which the fire of faith is made.) At the lecture which follows he does not even possess a sheet of paper on which to take notes, but immediately after it he reveals or boasts to some of his fellows that he has been to the office of arms to look up his family tree. "I know you are poor," he says frankly to Lynch, and shares his last cigarette with him. When a fat student says he has joined a field club to help his botanical studies Stephen says dryly, "Bring us a few turnips and onions the next time you go out to make a stew." When, thinking of his love, he lies in bed writing a villanelle, the contrasting squalor of his room is emphasized in the typical Joyceian way: masochistic as for himself, sadistic as for his character. He is distracted by a louse crawling on his neck, and "the life of his body, ill-clad, ill-fed, louse-eaten," makes him "close his eyelids in a sudden spasm of despair." Soon after, as he pauses outside Maples Hotel, its façade stings him "like a glance of polite disdain" and he imagines "the sleek lives of the patricians of Ireland housed in calm" and he derides the whole batlike race of serfs, kowtowing to these nabobs, to whom he belongs. Cranly now joins him and he mocks, to him, his father's position and his own circumstances. "Born," Cranly says sardonically, "in the lap of luxury." It is in this passage of arms with Cranly, who is intent on bringing him to realize his condition and compromise with it, that he utters his final arrogant decision to serve nobody but to achieve his ambition to be whole and free.

That we should find a strain of bitter anger in Joyce's nature is not surprising. He knows that his entire assets are his pride and his genius. His pride is boundless, and it is well that it should be, since a weaker man would have been wrecked by his circumstances. Granted this natural arrogance, his circumstances will serve only to dilate his pride and strengthen it. He has the courage of his genius. His squalid surroundings become his slave instead of his master. He will rise through them, beyond them, sublimate them by his art so that the gush and whir of the wings that surround Stephen that day on the strand at Dollymount are less like the mechanical whir of the wings of Daedalus than the whirring of the birds of inspiration about the head of the god Aengus which Mestrovic used as a proposed model for the Irish coinage and which Yeats seized on as the symbol of poetry or genius.

Let us pause at this famous passage. It is illustrative of Joyce's oscillation between outer and inner. It also measures the quality of *his* "moments of vision," his epiphanies or showings-forth, his manifestations of the inner truth of reality, of what Terence Hewett in *The Voyage Out* called the "what's behind things."

We note the setting for the passage. It occurs at the end of Chapter IV, which, we recall, opens with an account of Stephen's life after the famous Retreat. He has begun to order his life into a rosary of virtuous thoughts and acts; he has bound his hot flesh with the cincture of purity; he has submitted his mind to humility and piety. While he is in this mood, a Jesuit, in a striking passage, toying with a loop of cord from the window blind tries to lure him into the noose of the Order of Loyola. He returns to his home, described naturalistically, with the discarded crusts on the kitchen table and the lees of tea in the bottoms of the jam jars and jam pots that do service for cups in this impoverished household. There he finds his brothers and sisters, in the fading afterglow of the dying day, sitting tranquilly about the table singing, in their young, etiolated voices, that sad song of Tom Moore's, *Oft in the Stilly Night*. But though the scene is described in a naturalistic way, it is probable that we are expected to hear Joyce's fine tenor voice lingering over the words (which he does not print) that give inner significance to the moment.

> *The smiles, the tears of boyhood years,*
> *The words of love then spoken . . .*

or, sardonically:

> *I feel like one who treads alone*
> *Some banquet hall deserted . . .*

At this point we have entered the young man's mind again. We next find him on the wide strand at Dollymount on a lovely day of "dappled seaborne clouds." The Jesuit's temptation has passed. (In all Joyce we will note that *Pilgrim's Progress* is reversed. Satan is tempted by Christ, but surmounts him.) Why, Stephen asks himself, has he not surrendered to the priest's pleadings? The answer is not stated but is clearly given in the following naturalistic description of a "squad" of "Christian Brothers" with "uncouth faces" tramping back to their monastery. We again oscillate inwards when the sight of them raises "a faint stain of personal shame and commiseration in his own" face. (In that Ireland to be a Christian Brother was to be on about the same low intellectual level as a Plymouth Brother.) The clouds now dominate his mind, clouds blowing westward across the Irish Sea from Britain, from Europe, and they raise within him a confused music and old memories and names that gradually recede and merge into "a voice from beyond the world" calling him by his ancient name. Stephanos Dedalos. Bous Stephanoumenos. Bous Stephaneforos. . . . It is here at last that the image of the flying artificer rises in his mind, dispelling those melancholy images of lost boyhood that Tom Moore's song had evoked the night before.

> His soul had risen out of the grave of boyhood, spurning her graveclothes. Yes. Yes. Yes. He would create proudly out of the freedom and power of his soul, as the great artificer whose name he bore, a living thing, new and soaring and beautiful, impalpable, imperishable.

Just then comes the epiphany to which all this has been leading. He sees, as in a vision, a true showing-forth, a girl standing among the rock pools on long white legs, her thighs as soft-hued as ivory, her bosom as soft and slight as a dark-plumaged dove. The image informs and enchants him. He cries out in joyful profanity.

> Her image had passed into his soul for ever and no word had broken the holy silence of his ecstasy. Her eyes had called him and his soul had leaped at the call. To live, to err, to fall, to triumph, to recreate life out of life! A wild angel had appeared to him, the angel of mortal youth and beauty, an envoy from the fair courts of life, to throw open before him in an instant of ecstasy the gates of all the ways of error and glory.

We turn the page from that moment of release by revelation and we read: "He drained his third cup of watery tea to the dregs." The vision is mockingly and deliberately dispelled. But by this time we have long ceased to as much as think about "who thinks," or whether James is outside Stephen or within him. The very device, a commonplace of naturalism, used to break the moment of vision reinforces it by pity.

I will give one other example of the Joycean epiphany. It

is the key that opens and closes the final and most revealing section of the novel. Stephen, late for an English lecture, imagines the crowded lecture hall, and among the other students' skulls he imagines the skull of Cranly. It will be like the head of a priest appealing to the tabernacle for the other humble worshipers behind him. The following sentences then occur:

> Why was it that when he thought of Cranly he could never raise before his mind the entire image of his body but only the image of his head and face? Even now against the grey curtain of the morning he saw it before him like the phantom of a dream, the face of a severed head or death-mask, crowned on the brows by its stiff black upright hair as by an iron crown.

He goes on to elaborate a little his idea that Cranly is a fat priest, as it were a father confessor, and then:

> Through this image he had a glimpse of a strange, dark cavern of speculation but at once turned away from it, feeling that it was not yet the hour to enter it.

The remaining part of the book leads us steadily towards this cavern, which begins to open when Cranly and Stephen discuss religion and Stephen Diabolus rejects the last of his temptations, which, this time, revolves about Cranly's appeals to him to have pity on his mother. It is at the conclusion of this duel that Stephen makes his famous resolve to serve nothing in which he does not believe, home, fatherland or church, and to express himself "in some mode of life or art as freely as I can and as wholly as I can, using for myself the only arms I allow myself to use, silence, exile and

cunning." Then, apparently quite casually, this prolonged
and sinuous approach and conclusion is boiled down in his
diary to one single image. He compares Cranly to Saint John
the Baptist, the precursor of Christ (enemy of Stephen
Diabolus), in these words:

> Also when thinking of him saw always a stern, severed
> head or death-mask as if outlined on a grey curtain or veron-
> ica. [We recall that grey curtain of the morning some eighty
> pages back.] Decollation they call it in the fold. Puzzled for
> a moment by Saint John at the Latin Gate. What do I see?
> A decollated precursor trying to pick the lock.

"What do I see?" It is what Stephen Daedalus always sees:
not so much the actual person as the mirror in that person's
hand. What Stephen had seen at the entrance to his cavern of
speculation has been finally compressed into one image
which epiphanizes the function of that one person in his life:
Cranly, i.e., the worldly church, as the precursor picklock
of his soul.

I think we must agree that these moments of vision are
not the sort that illuminates life for Virginia Woolf. These
are moments infinitely expanded and fortified by Joyce's
awareness of the intellectual and moral content of all experience, giving to his narrative a force and a meaning far beyond that of mere aesthetic or sensory experience, radiating
out of an intense personal drama, which is also a metaphysical drama, in which the antagonists bear many names and
aspects — shame, pride, surrender, revolt, good, evil, faith,
unfaith, liberty, fraternization — all of them so many elements in the interpretation of the protean life-sense of one

satanically and triumphantly arrogant young Irishman bearing the banner with the device *Non Serviam.*

The point is that Joyce's epiphanies are, at their most effective, far more than naturalistic summaries, far more than tinglings along the nerves. They come from somewhere beyond
the actual of the there and the then, the external Dublin, the
overt reality. His mirror-bearers are men, but the images they
reflect are more than human, because they pierce into the
young man's depths where the struggle and the prize are
both superhuman. Recall the source of Mrs. Woolf's phrase
"moments of vision." It comes from Thomas Hardy's poem:

> *That mirror*
> *Which makes of men a transparency . . .*

Who, he asks, holds it to us?

> *That mirror*
> *Can test each mortal when unaware;*
> *Yea, that strange mirror*
> *May catch his last thoughts, whole life foul or fair,*
> *Glassing it — where?*

Are Mrs. Woolf's moments of vision intimations of things
beyond the flaming ramparts of the world?

> *All this was a long time ago, I remember,*
> *And I would do it again, but set down*
> *This set down*
> *This: were we led all that way for birth or death?*

Which was the first Epiphany. Are we, in Joyce, led from one
moment to another for birth or death? We will not rightly in

terpret his images if we think of them as mere illuminations on a psychological level.

If Joyce were merely a writer on that level he would not be the great literary hero of our time, would not have created a character that has caught the sympathy and imagination of the world. Daedalus is the persona, or mask, of a man who has handed back his ticket to the Almighty out of much more than human pity for the sufferings of humanity. He is a Promethean rebel defying nature and God by the extent and intent of his rejection. He reinvokes Camus's statement about the individualist — that he must reject reality in order to affirm his own existence. "He wanted," we are told of Daedalus, "to meet in the real world the unsubstantial image which his soul constantly beheld." Not finding it there, he will fly away, like his fabulous namesake, from and beyond the world. Joyce's flight from Dublin like Stephen's is only the symbol of a far greater flight. As Mr. Hugh Kenner has made so clear in his most percipient study *Dublin's Joyce* — to my mind the best thing written on Joyce, and to which I am much indebted in all this — Dublin was for James-Stephen a microcosm of a total divergence between man and God. In rejecting his native city and all it stood for, Joyce rejected his one fated field of life wherein he might have read the signatures of mortal things and made them tolerable, intelligible, meaningful. In their place he hoped to create, like a god, a new materiality. That splendidly blasphemous intent is to be found in his first novel, wherein he makes the absurd claim for himself, as an artist — which his whole work in fact belies — that the artist *can* be detached. "The personality of the artist . . . refines itself out of existence, impersonalises itself, so to speak. The aesthetic image in the dramatic form is life purified in and reprojected from the human imagination." So far we can go with him. But then: "The mystery of aesthetic like that of material creation is accomplished. The artist, like the God of the creation, remains within or behind or beyond or above his handiwork, invisible, refined out of existence, indifferent, paring his fingernails."

So far one cannot go with him, since the artist cannot but be, himself, as much involved in the act of creation as a man who makes bodily love to a woman and is reproduced in their child. To deny this is the ultimate revolt possible to man this side of suicide. The fascination of Joyce's denial is that he got away with it simply by recording the battle cry in the *Portrait* and the progress of the battle in *Ulysses;* and sometimes one feels that *Ulysses* also records the defeat, but if it does it records it so magnificently that the very record is yet another triumph. One must, however, utter a caveat. Joyce got away with it because he was Joyce. Nobody can imitate an autobiography. His books are unique and inimitable.

And though he got away with it he paid a dear price. There were certain limitations which no *Non Serviam* could overcome. He could record a revolt, but he could never go farther than the revolt. There could be no sequel to those first two books. He had, by his too total rejection, walked himself into an impasse. That impasse was that he rejected intellectually everything in which he was involved emotionally, like a man who rejects in his brain a woman he loves in his deepest being. He was too involved in his own embryo ever really to be free of it. His past haunts him like a succubus. He can talk of nothing else. The flight and the chase are unending, so that his work has no ending except the recurrent denial, the recurrent flight, the smashing of the chandelier to the old strangled cry of "With me all or not all. *Non Serviam . . . Nothing!*" And time's livid final flame leaps up and the ruin of all space. Or the ending is two old washerwomen by the Liffey falling into night and sleep. In the splendid effort to cast away everything old and to create something utterly new, he left himself with only one thing to write of, himself, child of Adam. Refusing to come to terms with the created world — which for him meant home, fatherland and church — he had no mechanism wherewith to come to terms with his own disconnected being, except, like so many other modern writers, ego-identification through revolt, which he then made the subject of fictionalized autobiography. It is why all his characters have only one function — to be his mirror-bearers.

It was from the viewpoint of literature a magnificent revolt, and one would not wish that it had not to happen, since the books won from it are so moving, so true and so revealing, not to mention so entertaining and so amusing. One cannot even wish that it had been less agonizing, that he had not had to suffer the meanness of Edwardian Dublin, the stupidities of the Irish Church, the puritanism of its priests, the total intellectual poverty of his teachers, the misery of his own poor home, the bitter loneliness of his ravaged youth in that little, remote, untutored, inexperienced, conquered, timid and emotionally besotted island on the rim of the world. For out of it all he got, at least, something worth struggling with, a pressure to which he had to respond or die, something terrible enough to be worth denying. In denying it he clarified himself. Before he finished with Ireland he at least knew what he did not believe in, and had inklings of what was worthy of a man.

As I copy out these pages I find Mr. J. B. Priestley asking, challengingly, what influence Joyce really had, and by way of a test asking if anybody could name twenty writers who show it. But, surely, the rebellious anti-Hero who is all over modern fiction must have been enormously encouraged to parade himself by the image of the arrogant revolt of Stephen Daedalus? The twenties were ripe for just such a leader. He was their bellwether. All those young men and women who were unhappy at school, who had had unkind or un-understanding fathers, had mother complexes, hated the society in which they grew, rebelled against convention, found themselves out on a limb, conspired against their elders, rejected tradition, who saw themselves, as Julien Sorel saw himself, forced to become disciples of Tartuffe and Napoleon, all those hypersensitive "sad young men" — who have become such a bore to us in the long run, largely because so few of them had the manliness of Daedalus — were largely inspired by Joyce. Not that Joyce invented the type or the idea. But he did resurrect in modern terms an appealing type. The anti-Hero, as I have shown in my Foreword, goes back a long way. From Don Quixote onward he has gone on reappearing in many guises: to think of a few at random, as Adolphe, Julien Sorel, Frédéric Moreau, Raskolnikov, almost any of Hemingway's lone wolves, de Rastignac, the son of *Father and Son;* he is the basis of *Les Faux-Monnayeurs;* he turns up in Duhamel, Romain Rolland, Marcel Aymé; Waugh poked fun at or through him; Greene introduced him to God; he is any of Miss Bowen's doomed heroines; he is all over Moravia's work; in Bloch, and Musil, and Svevo. But the list is endless.

He will probably always be with us now, or as long as youth believes in individual sincerity, and Ibsen's damned compact majority seems to betray it. The only places where he is not today are the territories of the Cowboy and the Private Eye.